JUAN de ONATE'S COLONY IN THE WILDERNESS

An Early History of the American Southwest

Robert McGeagh, Ph.D.

Sunstone Press
Santa Fe, New Mexico

ACKNOWLEDGEMENT

The author expresses his appreciation to
Senator Emilio Naranjo and the Rio Arriba County Commission
for encouraging the publication of this book as part of the
Onate Monument Project and the Columbus Quincentennial.

10 9 8 7 6 5 4 3 2

Printed in the United States of America

Library of Congress Cataloging in Publication Data:

McGeagh, Robert, 1934—
    Juan de Onate's colony in the wilderness : an early history of the
American Southwest / Robert McGeagh. -- 1st ed.
          p.   cm.
    Includes index.
    ISBN 0-86534-153-2 : $8.95
    1. Onate, Juan de, 1552-1627. 2. New Mexico—Discovery and
exploration. 3. New Mexico—History—To 1848. 4. Spaniards—New
Mexico—History. I. Title.
F799.M29 1990
978.9'01'092—dc20   90-49998
                                                                     CIP

Published in 1990 by SUNSTONE PRESS
        Post Office Box 2321
        Santa Fe, NM 87504-2321 / USA

For Nancy...mi otro Yo

Figure 1: Excavated ruins of San Gabriel, first Spanish capital in the Southwest. Archaelogy-Southwest Sites, Yuque-Yunque, San Gabriel File Collection, No. 12843. New Mexico State Records Center and Archives.

CONTENTS

ILLUSTRATIONS

PREFACE

The idea for this history of one of Europe's oldest American colonies originated in 1984 at a ticket desk in the Dallas/Fort Worth Airport where I had gone to pick up a pre-paid ticket to Albuquerque, New Mexico. When asked for identification, I presented my New Mexico's driver's license, only to be told that a Mexican license did not meet the airline's requirements. And earlier this year at a Community College convention in Seattle, Washington, I was listed as a "foreign visitor."

Similar stories of mistaken identity with our neighbor to the south are legion in New Mexico, prompting one author to refer to the region as the missing state and causing the state's automobile license plates to display the paranoid inscription: New Mexico, U.S.A. Consequently, I decided to contribute to New Mexico's quest for geographical integrity and tell the story of the origins of an ethnic heritage which is deeply woven into the warp and woof of today's America.

But if the geographical location of the state remains an enigma to many out-of-staters, its history remains even more illusive. Generally, American History books, taking inspiration from the purveyors of the Black Legend which depicted Spain as "the evil empire", gives only passing mention to the pervading influence of that country on this nation's past.

The American Southwest was coveted by early Spanish explorers for its potential mineral wealth for the State and for its abundant harvest of souls for the Church. Although the hopes for golden cities and riches beyond their wildest dreams were never fulfilled, the conquistadors of New Mexico left a legacy of prodigious achievements and sired a thriving population which today shares the bloodlines of both Spanish and Indian forbears.

The opportunity to relate the early history of New Mexico presented itself on the occasion of the commemoration of the Columbus Quincentennial scheduled for 1992. To mark the event, the Rio Arriba County Commission passed a resolution in March 1990 to erect a monument in honor of Don Juan de Onate, conquistador and colonizer of the region. To help promote public awareness and support for the project, I was asked to write a narrative history of the discovery, exploration and colonization of New Mexico.

Generations of Spanish conquistadors extended Columbus' work of discovery throughout the Western Hemisphere. Within forty years of the first landfall in the Caribbean, explorers and missionaries were trudging through the deserts and across the mountains of New Mexico in search of gold, silver and souls. Thus began the 'encuentro', the coming together of two disparate races and cultures to create a syncretistic fusion, a new race, which still preserves its Hispanic language and culture, and forms part of a unique mosaic of ethnic pluralism in 20th century America.

My story begins with the arrival of the first Europeans in New Mexico in the 1530s and ends with the completion of the discovery and settlement in 1700. For my facts I have relied on the standard sources, especially on the pioneering research of Ralph Emerson Twitchell in "The Leading Facts of New Mexican History" (published 1911) and the exhaustive documentary collections compiled by George P. Hammond and Agapito Rey in their 1953 study "Don Juan de Onate, Colonizer of New Mexico 1595-1628". Recent translations of Onate and de Vargas documents by John Kessel further illuminate the early period of American Southwestern History. But undoubtedly, the most dramatic and full account of the colonization is that of Onate's chronicler, Gaspar Perez de Villagra, whose epic poem describes the events of Onate's conquest of the Upper Rio Grande.

Among the many secondary sources contained in books, articles and monographs, I am particularly indebted to the work of Warren Beck, whose "New Mexico: A History of Four Centuries" still remains the best scholarly survey of the state's history.

On this occasion of the Columbus Quincentennial and the inauguration of the monument to Juan de Onate, I offer this overview of Spain's colony in the wilderness in hopes that it will shed some light on a vital historical period of our nation's past, and at the same time, help to dispel some popular misconceptions concerning the geographical location of the state of New Mexico, U.S.A.

Robert McGeagh, Ph. D.
Espanola, New Mexico
September 10, 1990

INTRODUCTION

When I was a boy growing up in Guachupange in the Espanola Valley in northern New Mexico, my father used to tell me stories of our ancestors who came to this valley on the Upper Rio Grande centuries ago. He told me of the great men of our past: the explorers Cabeza de Vaca and Coronado, and the colonizers Onate and de Vargas. I thrilled to the exploits of these Spanish conquistadors, and the sacrifices and hardships they endured to settle these lands in the American Southwest.

But when I attended school, the history books told me only of the first colonizers of the European settlements in the East, authentic heroes like Captain Smith, Sir Walter Raleigh and William Penn. Yet Juan Vasquez de Coronado explored this part of the future United States long before the English, Dutch and French settlements appeared along the Atlantic seaboard. However, U.S. history surveys continue to ignore the historic deeds of our Hispanic forbears. In a recently published edition of "A People and a Nation: a History of the United States" (1990,p16) the authors state: "Venturing northward (from Mexico), conquistadors like Juan Rodriguez Cabrillo, Hernando de Soto and Juan Vasquez de Coronado found little of value"—this in spite of the fact that, in his day, Coronado's detailed reports on the geography of the Southwest and his observations on the flora and fauna of the region ranked on a par with the later surveys of Lewis and Clark and Zebulon Pike.

And what of Juan de Onate? Although he definitively established the first European colony in the Southwest and began construction of the first capital, San Gabriel, on the west bank of the Rio Grande in 1598, he has long been denied his rightful place in the history of our country. Early in my political career I resolved that some day I would try to give the memory of Onate fitting recognition by constructing a lasting monument to the colonizer of the Southwestern United States. Now the time has come, and plans for the construction of a monument and visitor center dedicated to Juan de Onate are being implemented by the Rio Arriba County Commission. The complex is slated for completion during the Columbus Quincentennial in 1992.

One of the major goals of the project is to spread the knowledge of Juan de Onate and the colonization of New Mexico. To help realize that goal, Dr. Robert McGeagh has published this history of the discovery of New Mexico and its settlement by Onate. He tells the story of great men and the people who followed them into the remote and unreclaimed regions of the

American wilderness. Upon reading this narrative, one soon becomes aware of the bravery, tenacity and stubborn determination which drove our Hispanic ancestors to plant a durable culture in the wilds of the Southwest. It is a story of man's endurance in the face of a hostile environment, of great triumphs and equally great defeats.

In the ensuing centuries the descendants of these first colonists have flourished in the mountains and deserts of the Southwest, and today's Hispanic population forms one of the largest ethnic minorities in the U.S.A. Indeed, it is high time that we recognize the outstanding accomplishments of our Hispanic forbears and the creative role they played in the history of our country; thus, it is my fond hope that this story of the forgotten state of New Mexico and the monument to Juan de Onate will contribute significantly to that end.

Senator Emilio Naranjo
County Manager, Rio Arriba County,
New Mexico. August 1990

CHAPTER 1

THE DISCOVERY

The recorded history of New Mexico had its beginnings as the result of an event which occurred some 36 years after the discovery of the New World. In the year 1528, a Spanish ship was blown off course and wrecked near the site of present-day Galveston. The survivors were part of the ill-fated expedition to Florida of the Spanish conquistador, Panfilo de Narvaez. But Texas proved no more hospitable to the Spanish than Florida. Hunger, exposure and Indian attacks took their toll, drastically reducing the number of survivors to fifteen. Soon only four men remained of the hardy group of Spanish adventurers who had set out in search of God, Glory, and Gold.

One of these men, Alvar Nunez Cabeza de Vaca, was destined to be the first white man ever to set foot in New Mexico. He was accompanied by an Arabian slave of Morocco, Esteban (Estebanico). Cabeza de Vaca was typical of the Spaniards who came to the New World to make a fortune. Like other conquistadors, he was willing to endure fantastic hardships in pursuit of his goal. His eight-year odyssey through Texas and New Mexico has come down to us in the annals of the Conquest as a feat of endurance on a par with the exploits of more famous conquerors.

The four castaways began their westward trek unaware of the hazards that lay in store for them. Although their knowledge of the geography of the region was extremely primitive, they were sustained by the vague hope that somewhere to the west lay the frontier outposts of the Viceroyalty of New Spain. As they traveled westward through the trackless wastes of northern Texas, they repeatedly fell into the hands of various Indian tribes.

Their odyssey began to follow a pattern. The Indians first captured and enslaved the Spaniards. Gradually, however, due to their knowledge of European medicine and medical techniques, they won the confidence of their Indian captors and were given the respect due to healers and medicine men. Eventually, they either escaped or were granted their freedom by their admiring hosts. Upon being freed from one Indian group, they pushed westward only to be enslaved once again by another tribe. And thus the slow process of either escaping or winning their captors' confidence started all over again. Eventually, they made their way into southeastern New Mexico at a point close to the modern town of Carlsbad. They followed the Pecos

River for some distance before striking westward and crossing the Rio Grande near present-day El Paso. Finally, in 1536, they arrived at the northern Spanish garrison of Culiacan.

Dressed in skins and burnt by the sun and the wind, they presented a curious sight to the townspeople. But it was their stories of untold riches lying to the north which aroused the popular interest. Cabeza de Vaca was ordered to go to Mexico City to relate these wonders to the Viceroy, Antonio de Mendoza, the shrewd ruler of New Spain. De Vaca told him of the Seven Golden Cities that he had seen during his sojourn in the North. He spoke of large populations of sedentary Indians waiting to be converted to the Christian faith, and of signs of rich lodes of gold, antimony, iron, copper and other metals. These tales were enough to convince the Spanish authorities of the necessity of pushing beyond the warlike Chichimec Indians of northern Mexico and expanding the confines of New Spain to encompass the vast area which became known as New Mexico.

The sixteenth-century Spaniard was typified by Cervantes in the fictional Don Quijote de la Mancha and his companion, Sancho Panza. In these two individuals, Cervantes portrayed the Spanish character, at once practical, yet profoundly mystical. It was this schizophrenic trait which sent the hardheaded conquistadors chasing after chimerical legends: the Fountain of Youth, El Dorado, Quivira, and the Seven Cities of Cibola. In 1536, the reports of Cabeza de Vaca of the fabled golden cities in New Mexico quickly spread, firing the imagination of the youthful soldiers and adventurers of the Viceroyalty of New Spain. However, before launching a major expedition into the region, Antonio de Mendoza, an extremely cautious ruler, decided to send a fact-finding expedition northward to verify the truth of the reports.

His first step was to find a worthy leader of the proposed expedition. Cabeza de Vaca himself declined the offer and Estebanico, despite his qualifications, was precluded from commanding Spaniards due to his status as a slave and a non-Christian. After considering several alternates, Mendoza finally settled on a Franciscan friar who had had considerable experience among the Indians and possessed the physical stamina necessary for such an undertaking. He had accompanied the conquistadors to Santo Domingo and Peru and had reputedly walked from Guatemala to Mexico City to report to the Viceroy on the ill-treatment of Indians by conquistadors in South America. In his commission from the Viceroy, Fray Marcos was instructed to convey to the Indians of the North the promises of Charles V, King of Spain, that they would be treated humanely and that anyone who abused them would be severely punished. These promises, as subsequent events would prove, were more honored in the breach than in the observance. However, such instructions were no doubt given to the leader of the expedition in order to please the Spanish sovereign who was in the process of issuing the New Laws aimed at curtailing the abuse of Indian labor by unscrupulous conquistadors.

Fray Marcos was ordered to make detailed studies of the demographic characteristics of the area as well as to record the geography, flora, and fauna of the northern regions. After preliminary preparations, the friar, accompanied by Estebanico as guide, went north to the Spanish frontier town of Culiacan. There he consulted with the Governor, the youthful Don Vasquez de Coronado, who told him of his own ambition to make such an expedition—an ambition he would later realize in the famous 'entrada' into New Mexico in 1540.

Finally, on March 7, 1539, the expedition got under way. In a letter to Viceroy Mendoza, Coronado reported: "Fray Marcos, his friend (Fray Onorato), the Negro and other slaves and Indians whom I had given them departed after twelve days devoted to their preparations." From Culiacan northward along the trail blazed by de Vaca, the dour Fray Marcos, dressed in the Franciscan habit of coarse Zaragosa cloth, trudged along accompanied by a few impoverished Indian servants. In contrast, Estebanico, flaunting his promise of obedience, impatiently pressed ahead. Boasting the trappings and entourage of a rich man and decked out flamboyantly in feathers, plumes, turquoise, coral, and tinkling bells, the Moorish slave led his triumphal procession northward toward the tragic fate which awaited him.

Along the way, he proved to be a constant thorn in the side of his superior. Fray Marcos reported that he indulged in all manner of vice: drinking and carousing, practicing heathenish medicine rites and even simulating the Church's sacramental rituals by solemnly anointing the sick with the sign of the cross. As a consequence, Fray Marcos decided to detach himself as much as possible from the company of the Moor, instructing him to form the vanguard of the main party by several days distance. A simple code of communication was devised. The Moor was told that if he encountered a city of moderate size, he should send back by Indian messenger a cross the size of a man's hand. If he should sight a large city, he should send back two crosses. But if he should discover a city comparable to the great cities of the Aztec Empire, he should send back a large cross. In less than five days, an Indian messenger appeared bearing a cross the size of a man as an indication of the importance of Estebanico's findings. The messenger also conveyed to the priest the news that they were on the brink of the great discovery of the Cities of Cibola which were familiar to the Indians with whom Estebanico had made contact. And to lend credence to this claim, another messenger arrived forty eight hours later carrying an equally large cross and bearing the injunction from Estebanico that the friar should hasten to join him. Fray Marcos was suitably impressed and immediately set out to overtake the advance party.

But the friar was unsuccessful in his efforts to catch up with his recalcitrant guide; day after day, his party pushed ahead but they were unable to contact the illusive Moor. It has been suggested that Estebanico planned it so in the hopes of being the first to make the great discovery of the Golden Cities and thus win fame and fortune for himself. However, furious as he was with his wily subordinate, Fray Marcos was forced to admit in his subsequent account of the journey that Estebanico had smoothed the way for him. As he traveled from village to village, he was received with respect and provided with an abundance of food.

Finally, after several weeks of such progress, the friar's group encountered the remnants of Estebanico's scouting party. Wounded and disheartened, the survivors told the priest of how they had arrived at a marvelous city situated at the foot of a giant mound. Based on later computations this "city" must have been Hawikuh, one of the Zuni pueblos in western New Mexico.

But Estebanico and his entourage had not been well received. His messengers had been ordered out of the city and charged upon pain of death not to return. Perhaps the reasons for this hostile response to the Moor's peaceful overtures sprang from the fact that the Zunis had recently received news of Spanish slaving activities among Mexico's West Coast Indians. But Estabanico, throwing caution to the winds, scoffed at the threat and boldly marched up to the entrance of the pueblo. This act of defiance proved to be his undoing, for he was immediately taken captive and held for interrogation. Upon learning that two white men, representatives of a powerful king, were following, his interrogators believed him to be a spy for a hostile force and decided to kill him. They swiftly carried out the execution of the Moor and to prove he was not immortal as some Indians claimed, his body was chopped into little pieces and bits of bone and dried flesh were distributed among the neighboring tribes with the admonition to kill any intruder who should venture into their territory.

When he learned of Estebanico's grizzly fate, Fray Marcos hastened back to Mexico City with the dubious report that he had indeed seen the Cibola and had witnessed with his own eyes the brilliance of those Golden Cities as they reflected the light of the evening sun.

Why did Fray Marcos de Niza insist in his report to the Viceroy that he had discovered the Cities of Cibola? Some historians are of the opinion that the good friar was convinced that he had really viewed the fabled cities. After learning of Estebanico's murder, he claimed that he approached the Zuni pueblos and without alerting the inhabitants, cautiously viewed the towns from the safe distance of some nearby hills. Perhaps he saw the strings of corn drying on the flatroofed adobe houses and mistook the glint of the sun as reflecting gold. His fertile imagination was able to supply the rest of his story.

However, a more likely historical opinion states that Fray Marcos never actually saw New Mexico, but rather turned back before reaching the present international boundary line. Historians have presented convincing proof that he could not possibly have had time to cover the vast distances he claimed to have traveled. It has also been suggested by some scholars that maybe even Viceroy Mendoza himself was implicated in a plot to assure a subsequent major expedition and had instructed the friar to return from his fact-finding mission with a favorable report, irrespective of what he actually found in the North. Whether or not this was so, one fact is certain, the priest's report sparked exaggerated stories of his discoveries. According to a rumor which soon spread, the people of New Mexico wore belts of gold and had successfully domesticated camels, cows and even the mythical unicorn. The official outcome of Fray Marcos' report was a massive effort to prepare a major expedition under the leadership of Francisco Vasquez de Coronado, the youthful governor of Nueva Galicia. Its purpose would be the expansion of Spanish dominion into the 'terra incognita' of the northern regions.

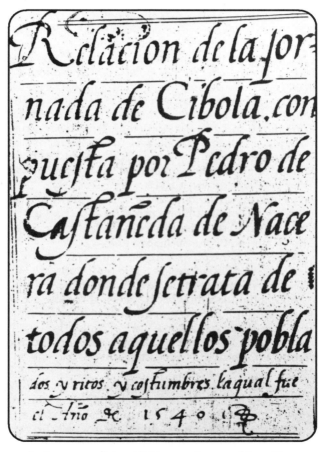

Figure 2: Account of the 1540 expedition of Don Francisco de Coronado, written by Pedro Castaneda de Nagera. Miscellaneous Spanish Archives. New Mexico State Records Center and Archives.

CHAPTER 2

THE EXPLORATION

Francisco Vasquez de Coronado had sailed to the New World with Viceroy Mendoza and possessed many influential friends at the Spanish court who could attest to his leadership abilities. But perhaps more important than his undoubted capabilities as a leader, was the fact that he was able to finance the proposed expedition. Spanish law dictated that the royal treasury would only provide for outfitting the contingent of priests designated to accompany the expedition and that all other costs must be borne by the sponsors of the venture.

Though himself only moderately wealthy, Coronado had married a rich woman whose fortune he proceeded to invest in outfitting his expedition. As far as he was concerned, this was to be money well spent, for the return on his investment in terms of gold, silver, land and Indian laborers would be worth the initial cash outlay.

All in all, it was a business venture with the profits to be shared in varying degrees by the investors. The estimated cost of the expedition in modern currency was about a million dollars.

Coronado found little difficulty in recruiting members for his enterprise. Young men, many of them still in their teens, pawned what few valuables they possessed in order to raise the money to pay for their personal equipment. Unemployed soldiers, adventurers and youthful grandees flocked to Compostela, the capital of Nueva Galicia, to join in the feverish preparations for the great expedition. They were inspired by visions of wealth and adventure which awaited them in New Mexico.

According to the most accurate estimates, the expedition was composed of approximately 235 Spaniards who possessed horses. They wore the steel or leather armor of the Spanish hidalgo and were armed with guns, crossbows and a variety of swords and daggers. Besides those fortunate enough to own horses, there were about 62 foot soldiers similarly accoutered and as many as 1,000 Indians accompanying the expedition as porters and livestock tenders. And since the expedition was a missionary enterprise as well as a business venture, a group of clerics accompanied the Spanish conquistadors under the tutelage of the ubiquitous Fray Marcos.

An air of optimism prevailed at Compostela, the preparations for the journey reflecting the gala spirits with which the young adventurers faced the future. Finally, with all preparations completed, Coronado led his expedition out of Compostela in February of 1540 on the first leg of the journey to New Mexico. Since he was anxious to reach the promised land with all possible haste, he left the slow-moving main force to proceed at a pace dictated by the leisurely progress of the herds of livestock and with a hand-picked group of Spaniards, clerics, and Indians, he rapidly forged ahead.

But as he went along the trail charted by Fray Marcos, the first doubts about the priest's veracity began to be felt by the scouting party. Instead of the smooth topography and friendly enclaves of Indians promised in the report of the friar, the Spaniards encountered extremely rough terrain, sparsely populated by a few unfriendly Indian tribes. Coronado, in his later report to the Viceroy, was moved to exclaim, "Everything the friar (Marcos) had said was found to be quite the reverse—the truth is that there are mountains which, however well the trail might be repaired, could not be crossed without great danger that the horses would fall over the cliffs."

In fact, in the course of his northward trek, Coronado lost a number of Indian servants as well as a large quantity of livestock which he had to abandon due to the hazardous conditions of the trail. Food in the form of maize was obtained along the way from nomadic Indians in exchange for a few cheap trinkets.

The disastrous condition of the trail northward was only the first of Fray Marcos' prevarications, as the conquistadors were soon to discover to their chagrin. The priest's reports had contained a geographical error which, in spite of the primitive knowledge of contemporary geography, was a major miscalculation resulting in a sizeable loss of the expedition's investments. According to FrayMarcos, new Mexico's cities of Cibola were contiguous with the Gulf of California. Consequently, Coronado had outfitted a naval expediton under the command of Hernando de Alarcon to proceed under sail to New Mexico with supplies for the land forces. Naturally, the sea captain never made contact with Coronado's expedition.

But further disappointments still lay ahead. The leader's advance party moved up the western coast of Mexico and entered what is now the United States through southwestern Arizona. When Coronado reached a point at the approximate location of the modern Interstate 40, he turned eastward entering New Mexico at its western boundary. By July of 1540, he at last came within sight of the "fabulous seven cities"—in reality, a miserable collection of mud huts. And in place of wealthy inhabitants weighed down with gold ornaments, there existed only a group of sedentary Indians who eked out a bare existence in the arid region of western New Mexico.

These Zuni, according to the best archeological and anthropological studies, were a composite pueblo people whose bloodlines mingled with various strains of the primitive inhabitants of the region. They were a strong and intelligent people steeped in a complicated mythology which integrated every aspect of life with their religion. However, although the Zunis represented a higher culture than the nomadic Indians of northern Mexico, their "cities" were a profound disappointment to Coronado and his men. Spanish visions of wealth and luxury were immediately dissipated upon viewing the six Zuni Pueblos. As the chronicler, Pedro de Castaneda reports: "When they saw the first village, which was Cibola, such were the curses that some hurled at Fray Marcos that I pray God may protect him from them."

But their recriminations against the mendacious friar had to be postponed. The Spaniards were met by the Zuni inhabitants with showers of arrows, stones, and other missiles. The village had received prior warning of Coronado's approach and preparations had been made to repulse the Spaniards with all the means at its disposal. A phalanx of some 300 Indian warriors armed with bows and arrows, clubs, and leather shields faced Coronado and his men. In the ensuing melee, the Spanish won an easy victory, although Coronado himself was wounded. Besides a face wound, an arrow had lodged in his foot, and his body was badly bruised as a result of being repeatedly struck by stones.

After several hours, Coronado's forces, calling on St. James and the Blessed Virgin, stormed the gate of the pueblo and managed to gain access to the town. The Zunis, realizing that the battle was all but lost, sued for peace and an armistice was declared. In a gesture of magnanimity, Coronado forgave them for waging war against him and changed the name of the village of Hawikuh to Granada in honor of the birthplace of the Viceroy. On August 3, he dispatched a report to Viceroy Mendoza, mentioning, among other things, that Fray Marcos had fabricated everything except the names of the cities. The report was sent to Mexico City under armed escort. At Coronado's bidding, Fray Marcos returned to Mexico with the escort, no doubt to escape the anger of the disappointed Spaniards who were ready to vent their wrath against the hapless friar.

But despite their disappointment at the absence of riches among the Zunis of western New Mexico, the Spaniards were determined to continue their quest for mineral wealth. Coronado ordered exploratory expeditions to be launched immediately in the hopes of discovering some evidence of the rumored deposits of gold and silver. One group under the command of Pedro de Tovar explored the Hopi area of Arizona; another force commanded by Garcia Lopez de Cardenas pushed westward and were the first Europeans to view the majesty of the Grand Canyon. However, no one found any trace of gold or silver.

Meanwhile, a band of Indians arrived at Coronado's headquarters at Granada with stories of riches lying to the east. The Indians came from the Pecos Pueblo and were led by their chief whom the Spanish nicknamed Bigotes. His tales of numerous pueblos and vast herds of buffalo that roamed the eastern plains convinced Coronado to outfit another scouting expedition under the command of Hernando de Alvarado.

Alvarado's eastward trek led him into the country of the Rio Grande pueblos. He erected a cross in one of the villages near present-day Albuquerque and was pleased when an Indian priest came forward and sprinkled corn meal on it. Mistakenly, Alvarado interpreted this gesture as an act of homage to the Christian symbol, whereas in reality it was an Indian ceremony to ward off the evil of the strange icon the white men had erected in the pueblo.

The scouting party proceeded up the Rio Grande valley, visiting the pueblos as far north as Taos. Everywhere they were well received and showered with gifts. Unfortunately, these first friendly encounters between Spaniards and Indians were destined to be disrupted by acts of harshness perpetrated by both sides. After visiting the Rio Grande pueblos, Alvarado marched southeast and arrived at the Pecos Pueblo where he was introduced to a Pawnee Indian whom the Spaniards dubbed "El Turco" and who offered to guide him to another fabled area—the mythical Quivira.

According to El Turco, the Indians of that wealthy region not only paved their streets with gold, but even fashioned water pitchers out of the precious metal. Furthermore, he insisted that he himself had formerly possessed gold ornaments, but had been robbed of them by the Pecos chief, Bigotes. The fact that El Turco was able to distinguish between gold and silver, lent credence to his tale. Once again, the Spanish imagination was fired with visions of untold riches, Hernando de Alvarado, apparently believing the tall tales, immediately hastened to inform Coronado of this happy turn of events.

In the meantime, Coronado had sent Cardenas to prepare winter quarters at the pueblo of Tiguex near the modern town of Bernalillo on the Rio Grande where the expedition prepared to settle for the duration of the harsh winter of 1540-1541. That fateful winter also heralded the beginning of endemic conflict between Indian and Spaniard as the normally peaceful Pueblo Indians rebelled against the heavy demands made on them by the Spaniards. The latter extorted supplies of food and clothing from the meager stock kept by the Indians and as a result, bitter fighting ensued during which many Indians were slaughtered. And as a salutary example of the futility of rebellion against their Spanish conquerors, several Indian captives were burnt at the stake. Obviously, such treatment was not conducive to fostering cordial relations between Spaniard and Indian, and the barbarities perpetrated by the conquistadors left a legacy of hatred for the Spanish among the Pueblo Indians of New Mexico which would take many years to erradicate.

At the end of that cold and hungry winter of 1541, Coronado decided to undertake the long journey to the east in search of Quivira. It was undoubtedly a brave proposal, for in addition to the unknown hazards of the terrain, the Spanish believed El Turco's story that they would encounter a powerful monarch in Quivira who ruled over a race of giants. But Coronado was a resourceful leader who enjoyed the loyalty and esteem of his men. And so with an entourage of 1500 Indian porters, he marched eastward with the imaginative El Turco as his guide. When he reached the Texas panhandle near modern-day Amarillo, he proceeded northward with fifteen soldiers at a more rapid pace, leaving behind his Indian bearers.

Meanwhile, the first suspicions of El Turco's mendacity were felt by the Spaniards. Groups of Plains Indians whom they met on their march, knew nothing of the reputed wealth of Quivira. And, furthermore, the other Indian guide, Isopete, insisted that El Turco had purposely deceived the explorers. Based on a subsequent confession extracted under torture, Historians have suggested that El Turco had slyly attempted to lure the Spaniards onto the great plains of northern Texas with the intention of abandoning them and leaving them to die of exposure on the trackless wastes. These doubts and premonitions concerning El Turco's integrity caused Coronado to issue an official order that the Indian guide was no longer to be trusted.

Unhampered by the slow-moving bearers, Coronado and his men made rapid progress and soon arrived on the plains of Kansas where their high hopes were once again dashed. At the present site of Lyons, Kansas, they reached Quivira. Like Cibola, it was a sorry sight: a collection of grass huts built in the shape of beehives. The race of giants turned out to be a rather primitive group of Wichita Indians who tattooed their bodies in accordance with some obscure religious ritual. Coronado, duped by the lies of his guide, unleashed his pent-up anger against the unfortunate El Turco. In accordance with rigorous Spanish law, the deceitful Indian was executed by garroting, a slow and excruciating form of strangulation.

After remaining in Kansas long enough to make some geographical explorations of the region and report on the fine quality of the soil, a disappointed Coronado led his men back to their headquarters at Tiguex. The negative information which he forwarded to the Viceroy on the absence of gold and silver in the areas he had surveyed, effectively curtailed further Spanish exploration of the Southwest for many years to come

Shortly after the expedition's return to Tiguex and after enduring another harsh winter, during which Coronado was severely injured in a fall from his horse, the decision was made to return to Compostela and abandon any further attempts at exploration in New Mexico.

But the missionary spirit of the Spanish clerics who accompanied the expedition would not be gainsayed; three priests and religious brothers decided to remain in New Mexico to begin the work of evangelizing the Indians. One friar, Juan de Padilla, even went back to the Wichita Indians of Kansas to carry the gospel message. Their missionary zeal was rewarded by execution at the hands of the Indians, but since they died while witnessing to their faith, Catholic doctrine teaches that their fate merited the "martyr's" crown and immediate entry into heaven. This guaranteed promise of eternal bliss was the spur that drove Spain's missionaries to face death in their initial efforts to spread Christianity.

The return of Coronado to Mexico in the Spring of 1542 was marred by failure. The sanguine predictions of New Mexican riches, the buoyant spirit and the contagious enthusiasm of the young adventurers that marked the beginning of the undertaking had been shattered amidst a plethora of hardships and disappointments. Immediately after the return of Coronado, recriminations, backbiting and accusations of incompetence began to fly back and forth. Coronado was brought to trial before the 'Audiencia' in Mexico City accused of mistreatment of the Indians and failure to adequately explore the region. Although he was acquitted of the charges, he never quite got over his disappointment and the physical wounds he had suffered during his sojourn in New Mexico. After a lingering illness, he died at the early age of forty-four. As the chronicle states: "Francisco Vazquez de Coronado died and passed from this present life on the night of Saturday which was accounted the 22nd day of September of this year 1554".

With the passing of Coronado, New Mexico receded into the background of Spain's New World policy. His failure to bring back evidence of rich deposits of gold and silver cooled the official ardor for further expeditions into the northern region.

CHAPTER 3

THE EXPEDITIONS

After the Coronado expedition of 1540, interest in New Mexico waned for a period of forty years. In the meantime, Spain's efforts to extend its territory north of the settled areas of Mexico continued. With the discovery in 1546 of silver mines in Zacatecas and southern Chihuahua, colonists poured northward to establish the new province of Nueva Viscaya. The Indians of the region provided a readily available labor supply; against their will they were rounded up by Spanish slavers and forced to work in the mines. Frontier towns such as Santa Barbara came into existence, possessing all the lawless characteristics of the typical mining camp. Miners, slave hunters, fugitives from justice and vagrants drifted northward to the frontier of New Spain. Among this motley assembly of Spaniards, Indians and Mestizos were small groups of Franciscan friars eager to penetrate further north in search of souls and, 'deo volente', the "martyr's crown".

One of their number, Agustin Rodriguez, a lay brother, petitioned the Viceroy for permission to explore the north country for purposes of missionary work. It is noteworthy that permission for this type of expedition was readily given by the Spanish authorities. The old treasure hunting expeditions had fallen into disrepute as being wasteful of men and resources. Furthermore, the Spanish Monarch, Philip II, a devout Catholic, was importuning his New World representatives to further the cause of Christianity in those lands within their jurisdiction. Thus, for the rest of the sixteenth century the missionary motive was destined to supplant purely economic motivations for the conquest and colonization of New Mexico.

In this venture, Fray Rodriguez was joined by two other Franciscans: Fray Francisco Lopez and Fray Juan de Santa Maria. Nine soldiers were assigned to the party under the captaincy of Francisco Sanchez Chamuscado. In company with nineteen Indians, the group set out from Santa Barbara on June 5, 1581. They traversed the Rio Conchos and arrived at the Rio Grande from whence they proceeded northward as far as Coronado's old headquarters at Tiguex.

On the whole, the missionaries and their escort acted with restraint and were well treated by the Indians of the Rio Grande pueblos. However, the latter had not forgotten the harshness of the Coronado expedition and soon demonstrated their ingrained hatred of the Spanish. The occasion to vent their wrath on the intruders arose when Fray Juan de Santa Maria decided to return to Mexico to report on the progress of the expedition and to recruit more volunteers for their missionary endeavor. Foolishly, he decided to attempt the journey alone. But some Tano Indians, fearing that the priest intended to bring back more of the hated Spanish to New Mexico, waylaid and murdered him in Tijeras Canyon. When the other members of the expedition heard of the friar's fate, they renamed the village from which he had departed, El Pueblo del Malpartido.

Perhaps it was the fear that a similar fate awaited the rest of them which prompted the decision of Chamuscado to return to Mexico in April, 1582. However, the two Franciscans chose to remain behind and were summarily assassinated by the Indians after the departure of the military escort. Chamuscado himself fell ill on the trail homeward and died before reaching Mexico City.

The survivors of the expedition made their report to the Viceroy. They stressed especially the heavy concentration of Indians in New Mexico ripe for the missionary harvest. And to further edify the representative of the pious king, they recounted how they had given Saints names to various New Mexico pueblos.

With the return of this expedition, New Mexico once more became the topic of conversation and speculation among the inhabitants of New Spain. The disappointments of the Coronado years were easily forgotten, and would-be adventurers—once again converting rumor into fact—spoke of the riches to be gained in New Mexico. The King himself was impressed with the potential for evangelization and ordered the Viceroy to begin colonization procedures. However, before the ponderous official machinery could be set in motion to organize and outfit a colonizing expedition, rumors of the deaths of Friars Rodriguez and Lopez who had remained in New Mexico reached the frontier outposts of northern Mexico. These reports provided an immediate incentive to send out a small expedition to inquire further into the fate the two clerics.

Colonization plans for New Mexico received added impetus as a result of this expedition. Upon its return, exaggerated reports were published estimating the Indian population at 250,000. The leader of the expedition was hoping for a royal charter to establish a Spanish colony in New Mexico and consequently tailored his report in such a way as to favor his candidacy as official colonizer.

The author of these questionable statistics was a rich Spaniard, Antonio de Espejo, who had come to New Spain in 1571 as an official of the dreaded Inquisition. Subsequently, he had become a wealthy cattle—rancher in Queretaro, but had fallen afoul of the law when he murdered one of his 'vaqueros' in a fit of anger. Seeking refuge, he fled to the frontier of New Spain to evade the peace officers of the Spanish crown. While he was hiding out in this lawless region, he devised a scheme to help the Franciscans finance their expedition to New Mexico and thus to curry favor with the Spanish authorities. His offer was timely and provided the necessary funds to outfit the Franciscan expedition.

After some initial difficulty in obtaining a license for the undertaking due to the unsavory background of Espejo, the expedition set out from the Valle de San Gregorio on November 10, 1582. Officially, the group of two friars, fifteen soldiers and the usual contingent of Indians was under the authority of the Franciscan friar, Bernardino Beltran. However, in the absence of any clear directives from the governor of Nueva Viscaya, Antonio de Espejo was designated by the members of the expedition to take command.

Espejo and his men rode northwards following the basic route of the Rodriguez—Chamuscado expedition. They passed the Spanish slaving-station at El Jacal and the burial place of Chamuscado, eventually arriving at the Pueblo country in February 1583. Meanwhile, all hopes for the survival of Friars Rodriquez and Lopez were dispelled when definite word reached the expedition of their assassination at the hands of the Indians. Upon learning of their fate, Father Beltran urged the group to return immediately to Mexico. Espejo, however, was able to prevail upon the expeditionaries to proceed into New Mexico with the promise of the rewards that awaited them in the form of gold and silver.

The Spanish chronicler, Diego Perez de Luxan, gives the most trustworthy and detailed account of the expedition. Espejo, anxious to test reports of mineral deposits, journeyed in a westerly direction, ritualistically claiming all the territory in the name of the King of Spain. One of the phenomena which Luxan claims impressed the Spaniards, was the sky city of Acoma situated atop a high mesa and impregnable to outside attack. Further west, the expeditionaries discovered a stream which they named El Rio de los Reyes. And close by, they came across some mines which according to Luxan were "so worthless that we did not find in them any trace of silver, as they were copper mines and poor".

Espejo and his men penetrated as far as the Hopi pueblos in Arizona before retracing their steps to the Rio Grande. Along the way they were treated with grudging respect by the Indians. However, on more than one occasion, they were forced to do battle with hostile Indians whom they invariably defeated, garroting the prisoners to discourage further rebellion.

On the return .journey to Mexico, the expedition divided into two groups. One accompanied Fray Beltran, following the route of former expeditions along the Rio Grande; the other group, led by Espejo, went as far west as the Pecos Pueblo, returning to Mexico by way of the Rio de Las Vacas (Pecos River). Continuing southwest, they reached Santa Barbara in September 1583.

Upon his return, Espejo published his account of the expedition in October 1583, while the events were still fresh in his memory. As early as 1587, his narrative was translated into English and published in London under the title: "The Voyage of Anthony of Espeio, who in the years 1583, with his company discovered a Lande of 15 Provinces".

But in spite of the publicity afforded the expedition, Espejo himself did not receive the coveted charter to colonize the region. Other contenders with more influence at the Spanish court were competing for the honor of being the first to lead settlers into the northern regions of "La Tierra Nueva", now definitively referred to in official documents as "el Nuevo Mexico".

The chain of Spain's authority, reaching from Madrid to New Spain, was a bureaucrat's delight. Los Reyes Catolicos, Ferdinand and Isabela, had succeeded in creating a patrimonial and centralized monarchy which united the disparate provinces of "Las Espanas". With little diminution of power, royal authority spread to the colonies in the person of the Viceroy who ruled in the King's name. In turn, the Viceroy delegated his power through a series of agencies and individuals to the humblest 'Alcaldes' in the far-flung outposts of the empire.

The most important entity in the chain of command was the Council of the Indies. The Council drafted and issued American laws and served as the appelate judicial court for civil cases arising in the colonies. All decisions affecting the course of the empire passed through the Council's hands. It tended to be extremely meticulous and bureaucratic, weighted down with massive quantities of reports, laws, opinions, briefs and records. Usually, the Council mirrored the character and attitudes of the various reigning monarchs. And so in the last decades of the 16th century, the supreme Council of the Indies was disposed to colonize the marginal areas of the empire for missionary purposes.

In response to Espejo's report which had stressed the potential for evangelization, the king issued a royal' cedula' (decree) on April 19th, 1583, authorizing the conquest and colonization of New Mexico. It was stated in the charter that the Council of the Indies would oversee the arrangements in accordance with custom. Furthermore, the entire enterprise must be privately financed with no cost to the Crown.

Due to the top-heavy bureaucracy characteristic of Spain's imperial rule and the consequent inefficiency of the colonial system, a period of over ten years elapsed before the march northward finally got under way. Meanwhile, there was no lack of applicants for the coveted charter to enter into contract with the Crown for the pacification and settlement of the northern regions. But while the various candidates wasted time vying with each other for the King's favor, two illegal expeditions were launched which intentionally bypassed the official process.

The first of these 'entradas' was led by Gaspar Castano de Sosa, the Lieutenant-Governor of Nuevo Leon. He took it upon himself to interpret a Spanish law which stated that any governor had the right to colonize lands already discovered. Without waiting for an official interpretation, Castano de Sosa prevailed upon the entire population of the mining town of Almaden to accompany him in search of richer mines rumored to exist in New Mexico. His entire colony, consisting of 170 men, women and children, proceeded northward and reached the Pecos Pueblo in December, 1590. After clashing briefly with the Indians of the pueblo, Castano de Sosa led his colony to the Rio Grande and selected an area near the pueblo of Santo Domingo for his new municipality.

But the colonists from Nuevo Leon proved to be a contentious lot and their bickering over Indian labor threatened to disrupt the fledgling colony. However, Castano de Sosa seems to have been an insightful leader, for he was successful in preserving the peace within his domain. Nevertheless, the colony was doomed because of its illicit character. When the Viceroy was apprised of its existence, he dispatched fifty troops under the command of Juan Morlete to arrest Castano de Sosa. When Morlete arrived in New Mexico, the colonists bowed to Spanish authority and docilely returned to their former homes in Almaden. Castano de Sosa was returned to Mexico under armed guard to face charges of illegally attempting to colonize New Mexico. The unfortunate first "Governor" of the province was found guilty and sentenced to exile in China. On his way there, he was murdered during a mutiny of galley slaves in the Moluccas. Subsequently, the charges against him were reviewed, and he was posthumously exonerated by the High Court.

It is indeed unfortunate that Castano de Sosa's venture came to so tragic an end. By all accounts, he was an able Governor, noted for his success in establishing friendly relations with the Indians of New Mexico. His qualities of tact and discretion enabled him to handle potentially explosive situations among his colonists with consummate skill. And his reports on the Indians, the land and the growth potential of the northern regions proved to be the most accurate to date.

In contrast to the seriousness of the Castano de Sosa enterprise, the illegal expedition of Francisco Leyba and Antonio Gutierrez de Humana stands out in the history of the period as one of the most brutal and sanguinary episodes of that whole bloodthirsty era. The account of their irresponsible journey was given by one of the Indian servants who had escaped under cover of night and told a story of violence and bloodshed. On their way to the buffalo plains in eastern New Mexico, the leaders fell into a vehement argument which resulted in the stabbing death of Leyba. Shortly thereafter the entire party was set upon by a band of marauding Indians and brutally massacred.

When Onate set out for New Mexico a few years later, the fate of the Humana-Leyba expedition was not yet officially known and he carried with him instructions to bring those men to justice. Meanwhile, the legal proceedings had been completed and Juan de Onate was given the royal commission to colonize New Mexico.

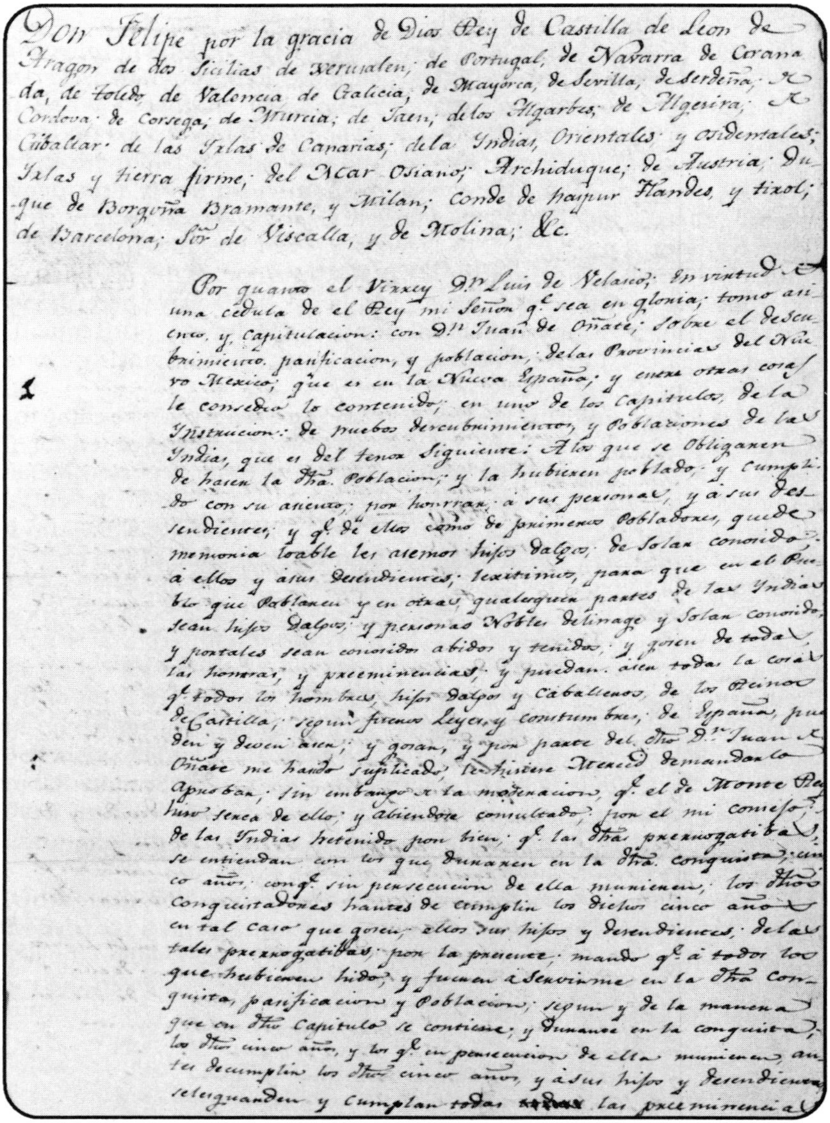

Don Felipe por la gracia de Dios Rey de Castilla de Leon de Aragon de las Sicilias de Jerusalen, de Portugal, de Navarra de Corana da, de Toledo de Valencia de Galicia, de Mayorca, de Sevilla, de Serdeña, de Cordova, de Corsega; de Murcia; de Jaen; de los Algarbes, de Algecira, de Gibraltar; de las Islas de Canarias; de las Indias, Orientales y occidentales; Islas y tierra firme, del Mar Osiano; Archiduque; de Austria; Duque de Borgoña Bramante, y Milan; Conde de flapsur Flandes, y tirol; de Barcelona; Señor de Viscalla, y de Molina; &c.

Por quanto el Virrey D.n Luis de Velasco; en virtud de una cedula de el Rey mi Señor q.e sea en gloria; tomo assi ento, y capitulacion: con D.n Juan de Oñate; sobre el descubrimiento, pasificacion, y poblacion, de las Provincias del Nuevo Mexico; que es en la Nueva España; y entre otras cosas le concede lo contenido; en uno de los Capitulos, de la Instruccion: de nuevos descubrimientos, y Poblaciones de las Indias, que es del tenor Siguiente: A los que se Obligaren de hacer la d.ha Poblacion; y la hubieren poblado; y cumplido con su asiento; por honrrar, a sus personas, y a sus descendientes; y q.e de ellos como de primeros Pobladores, quede memoria loable les hacemos hijos dalgos, de solar conocido, a ellos y a sus descendientes, legitimos, para que en el Pueblo que Poblaren y en otras qualesquier partes de las Indias sean hijos dalgos, y personas Nobles de linage y Solar conocido, y portales sean conocidos abidos y tenidos; y gozen de todas las honrras, y preeminencias; y puedan, hacer todas la cosa q.e todos los hombres, hijos dalgos y Caballeros, de los Reinos de Castilla; segun fueros Leyes y costumbres, de España, pueden y deven hacer; y gozan, y por parte del d.ho D.n Juan de Oñate me haveis suplicado; lo hiciere Merced demandando lo apuntaban; sin embargo de la moderacion, q.e el de Monte Rey tiene hecha de ello; y aviendose consultado; por el mi consejo, de las Indias teniendo por bien; q.e las d.has prerogativas se entiendan con los que duraren en la d.ha conquista; en años, conq.e sin persecucion de ella municien; los d.hos Conquistadores havian de cumplir los d.hos cinco años en tal caso que gozen ellos sus hijos y descendientes, de las tales prerogativas; por la presente; mando q.e a todos los que hubieren hido; y fueran a servirme en la d.ha conquista, pasificacion y Poblacion; segun y de la manera que en d.ho Capitulo se contiene; y duraren en la conquista q.e los cinco años, y los q.e en persecucion de ella municien, an de cumplir los d.hos cinco años, y a sus hijos y descendientes se les guarden y cumplan todas las preeminencias

Figure 3: Letter to Don Juan de Onate from Viceroy Luis de Velasco, promulgating the decree conferring the noble titles of Hijosdalgos on the first colonizers of New Mexico. Spanish Archives of New Mexico 1. No. 1087. New Mexico State Records Center and Archives.

CHAPTER 4

THE COLONIZATION

"Of Arms I sing,
and of that
heroic son
of his wondrous
deeds and of
his victories won."

So runs the first words of the epic poem written by Gaspar Perez de Villagra, Onates's historian and ardent admirer. The historical ballad was published in the year 1610, a decade before the Pilgrims landed on the shores of North America.

Contrary to popular belief, Juan de Onate was not born in Spain, but was the scion of a wealthy New World family. His father, Cristobal Onate, the Lieutenant-Governor of Nueva Galicia, had made his fortune as a developer of the silver mines in Zacatecas. Juan was a true product of the New World and had married the daughter of Hernan Cortez and the Emperor Montezuma's daughter. As Villagra states in his chronicle: "Juan de Onate was the husband of the great grand-daughter of the last of the Mexican kings and the granddaughter of the Marquis (Cortez)".

In all probability, Juan was born in 1552. Although little is known of his early life, it can be surmised that he received the typical upbringing of the sons of Spain's hidalgos. Religious education played an important part in the formation of the sons of the nobility, who were placed under the tutelage of venerable friars. This fact may account for the piety so evident among Spain's leaders in spite of their monumental excesses and moral lapses.

When Onate became a contender for the charter to colonize New Mexico, he was in the prime of his life. He had married a wealthy woman, Dona Isabel de Tolosa, the daughter of one of his father's rich partners. Most of his adult life had been spent in military pursuits and in prospecting for silver. On September 21, 1595, he was given the long-awaited authorization granting him the leadership of Spain's colonizing venture into New Mexico.

Preparations for the long trek north immediately got underway. As Villagra reports in canto six of his poem: "Soldiers flocked to enroll under

Onate's banner. They came like gallant courtiers assembling for some gay tourney, or like bees which, when April breezes blow, fill the air...Many sold all their worldly goods that they might fit themselves properly to enlist under the banner he raised". News of the expedition was proclaimed publicly in the streets and plazas of the cities and towns of New Spain.

Soon, however, the feverish preparations were halted with the arrival of a new Viceroy, the Count of Monterey, who countermanded Onate's commission. He did so on hearing reports circulated by Onate's rivals that he was incompetent and unsuited to command such an important undertaking.

The slander obviously had its desired effect for the Spanish King addressed a letter to "my Viceroy, The Count of Monterey, Governor and Captain-General of New Spain" revoking the permission given to Onate. Apparently, a rival claimant for the honor, Don Pedro Ponce de Leon, had powerful support at the royal court and was favored by the Council of the Indies. The Viceroy duly conveyed the King's command to Onate which stated that "the said Don Juan de Onate shall obey this my command, to halt and not advance any further from the point and place where he may be notified until new orders come from his Majesty".

These interminable delays had a deleterious effect on the morale of the prospective colonists who became dispirited and resentful. Villagra described the scene: "The army was dwindling away, the priests were leaving and the children of the colonists were wandering about the camp like lost cattle". Finally, after almost three years of vacillation and irresolution, Philip II authorized the viceroy to permit Onate to proceed with the colonization of New Mexico. And so in January, 1598, the expedition finally made ready to depart from the staging area at Santa Barbara in the province of Nueva Vizcaya.

By the terms of the royal charter, Onate was given the civil title of Governor and the military rank of Captain-General. Also, the prestigious title of 'Adelantado' was conferred upon him to signify his status as a conquistador. In the absence of easy communication between the proposed colony and the viceregal palace in Mexico City, Onate was deputed to exercise supreme control over his colonists. He was empowered to grant allotments of Indian laborers to the settlers, an institution known as the 'repartimiento.' Further, he had the authority to dispense grants of land— 'mercedes'—in accordance with customary Spanish land laws. In addition, he would receive a salary of six thousand ducats out of which he was expected to pay his travel expenses and personal taxes. By any standard, that was not a princely sum and the penury of the New Mexican governorship soon opened the door to corruption and malfeasance in office. As was the custom, the expenses of the entire expedition had to be financed by the grantee and Onate was forced to dig deeply into the family fortune. The Crown absorbed the cost of sending the Church's representatives, a contingent of mendicant friars, to accompany the expedition.

The men and women who set out with Onate to colonize New Mexico represented a cross-section of New World society and were by no means ethnically homogeneous. Many of these first settlers were 'mestizos,' the inevitable result of over seventy years of intermarriage between Spaniards and the indigenous inhabitants of New Spain. Spanish law was not adverse to such a mingling of blood-lines and social prejudice did not inhibit mixed marriages. In fact, the King had actively encouraged New World immigrants, the vast majority of whom were men, to intermarry with the Indians. A law was drafted under pressure from churchmen who deplored the irregular unions between Spanish males and Indian women, granting free land to those who legitimized their concubinage according to Catholic ritual. Spain's laws referring to 'limpieza de sangre'—purity of blood—were concerned with dogma rather than with racial purity, for the absence of the taint of heresy, as embodied in the doctrines of Judaism and Islamism, was important in defining a person's origins.

Besides the mestizo element among Onate's settlers, there were many soldier-adventurers from the Spanish mainland. Due to the dearth of Spanish unmarried women in the New World, the single male colonists would soon find wives among the Pueblo Indians of New Mexico, forming the basic Indo-Hispanic society of the region. Also, in the company of the Spaniards were several "foreigners", notably some Portuguese and even a solitary Greek.

By contemporary standards, the expedition was an enormous undertaking. Officially it was composed of 170 families and 230 single men. Among the latter were listed ten Franciscans, eight priests and two lay brothers; no one bothered to count the Indians who accompanied the expeditionaries. Each individual had to make a declaration of his possessions before the royal inspector, and these records are still extant in the 'Archivo de las Indias' in Sevilla. In scrutinizing the entries made by the royal inspector in the muster-roll of the expedition, it is interesting to note the various gradations of wealth among the colonists. Some of the young adventurers possessed no more than the clothes on their backs, while some of the more affluent settlers could boast an assortment of material possessions such as horses, armored saddles and harquebuses.

The expeditionaries brought with them eighty wagons—'carretas'—and seven thousand head of stock. The huge caravan is said to have stretched for four miles, and was divided into three or four sections which travelled five or six miles per day, each group maintaining a twenty four hour interval from the next, so as not to deplete the water supply in the water holes along the route.

The expedition followed the Conchas River for a short distance before striking across the arid deserts of Chihuahua. The caravan was constantly plagued by a lack of water and was always under threat of Indian attack. But Onate demonstrated his qualities of leadership by rallying the flagging spirits of his followers with impassioned rhetoric. Villagra reports that: "Our general, like Julius Caesar...leaped upon a prancing charger, rode before his men and cried 'Come, noble soldiers, knights of Christ, here is presented the finest opportunity for you to show your mettle and courage and to prove that you are deserving of the glories which lie in store for you'".

On April 20, 1598, Onate's colonists finally reached the 'Rio del Norte' (Rio Grande) about fifteen miles below the modern city of El Paso. After many days without water, the sight of the river seemed almost miraculous to the parched travellers. Both they and the livestock were so dehydrated from traversing the Chihuahua desert that many succumbed to the temptation to overindulge their thirsts. Villagra graphically describes the scene by the river: "The gaunt horses approached the rolling stream and plunged headlong into it. Two of them drank so much that they burst their sides and died...Our men, consumed by the burning thirst, their tongues swollen and their throats parched, threw themselves into the water and drank as though the entire river did not carry enough to quench the terrible thirst".

In a formal ceremony, Onate took possession of the territory in the name of the King of Spain. At no time did it ever occur to the conquistadors that their claim was anything but legitimate. Had not the Pope himself divided the newly discovered lands into two halves by the Treaty of Tordesillas: one half to Portugal, the other to Spain? The fact that the northern European Protestant countries would challenge this claim had no power to alter the conquistadors' stubborn conviction that they were entitled to all new lands west of the line of Tordesillas. Of course the rights of the Indians were pointedly ignored and did not even enter into the purview of these European controversies.

Thus, on the Feast of the Ascension, April 30, 1598, Onate took possession of all the kingdoms and provinces of New Mexico in the name of King Philip of Spain. His words succinctly epitomize Spain's world-view and medieval concept of man and nature. In a letter to his sovereign, Onate wrote: "Another reason (for the conquest of New Mexico) is the need for correcting and punishing the sins against nature and against humanity which exist among these bestial nations and which it behooves my King and Prince as a most powerful lord to correct and repress...Another reason is the great number of children born among those infidel people who neither recognize nor obey their true God and Father". With these words, Onate claimed sovereign rights to all the territories and "of its kingdoms contiguous thereto".

To mark the occasion, the expeditionaries were granted a day of rest and festivities. Starting with the 'Te Deum', the Church's hymn of gratitude to God, and a solemn High Mass, the colonists celebrated the festival with foot races and other competitive sports. One of Onate's captains, Marcos Farfan, even wrote a play which was staged for the entertainment and edification of the expeditionaries. The drama portrayed the eagerness with which the Indian population would receive the Franciscan friars and petition them for the saving waters of the sacrament of Baptism. It also graphically showed how Onate would readily overcome all resistance in his conquest of those territories.

A few days later, the caravan crossed the Rio Grande a few miles south of the modern metroplex of El Paso-Juarez. Following the course of the river, they arrived at the southernmost Indian settlement, the Pueblo of Teipan which is now extinct, as also is the language of the Piro Indians who inhabited the region. Because of the hospitality which these people extended to the colonists, they renamed the pueblo 'Nuestra Senora del Socorro', Our Lady of Help.

As they moved from one pueblo to another along the Rio Grande, the Spaniards introduced another peculiar institution, the 'requerimiento.'

Figure 4: San Juan Pueblo and Plaza, 1906. Bureau of Immigration Collection, No. 12070. New Mexico State Records Center and Archives.

Essentially, this consisted of a statement solemnly read to the Indians explaining that the King of Spain owned all their territory and they must submit to his rule; furthermore, they must accept Christianity, recognizing Catholicism as the only true religion and promising to obey its dogmas and moral laws. In return for their allegiance to Spain and its Christian God, they would be protected from their enemies in this world and assured a high place in the glorious life which awaited them in the world to come. Although there is little question that such medieval philosophizing was beyond the ken of those pueblo cultures, the Spanish were deadly serious in their intent. But the blandishments of Iberian Christianity came disguised in a gloved fist. If the Indians proved to be unreceptive to these salvific promises, the conquerors felt justified in waging a "just war" against them, burning their villages and putting men, women and children to the sword.

Doubtlessly, the fear of such dire consequences did more to assure Indian submission to the 'requerimiento' than the threats of hell fire and eternal damnation. Villagra was definitely convinced of the righteousness of the Spanish cause and even noted how nature collaborated with Christianity in a spectacular show of support for the friars' teachings: "As the party with saintly priests who brought the Holy Faith to combat and overthrow the forces of idolatry approached the pueblo, the elements it seemed clashed in terrible combat, for the sky became darkened with heavy black clouds and the entire earth shook and trembled as with the force of a mighty earthquake...God took compassion on us and deigned to hear their (the friars) saintly prayers...the inhabitants saw us approaching and all came forth and welcomed us, showing great reverence for the crucifix".

The tenacity with which the Spanish pursued their spiritual goals was duplicated in their zeal to attain their material objectives. By August, 1598, the colonists had established themselves at the pueblo of Yuque-Yunque on the east bank of the Rio Grande above Espanola, near the junction of the Rio Grande and the Chama rivers. They renamed the neighboring pueblo of Tewa Indians, 'San Juan de Los Caballeros' in honor of St.John the Baptist.

But the makeshift settlement at Yuque-Yunque was plagued with insects and rodents and soon proved inadequate for living purposes. Although the colonists had already begun construction of irrigation ditches and a church at the site, detailed plans were laid for the building of a permanent town on the west bank of the Rio Grande opposite the old pueblo. The embryonic settlement was named San Gabriel.

Unlike the Spanish peninsular towns, the proposed capital of New Mexico was carefully planned and designed according to a grid-iron pattern. The inspiration for this design had come from the neo-classical books on town planning which were current in 16th century Europe. The characteristic Spanish-American town consisted of a central plaza surrounded by government offices, the residence of the Governor or the Alcaldé Major,' the church and the principle commercial establishments.

Based on property holdings, social classes distributed themselves outward from the plaza, the persons of highest rank and greatest wealth occupying positions closest to the center; thus, the largest houses, the "palaces", the cathedral and the public buildings were clustered in the vicinity of the main 'plaza.' On the outskirts of the town, buildings were smaller and less impressive, while still further afield lay the sprawling Indian 'barrios,' haphazardly housing the marginal elements of society. San Gabriel followed the general pattern of uniform rectangular block construction. Twelve years later, in 1610, when the first capital was abandoned, the new town of Santa Fe would be constructed in strict conformity with New World city planning.

To celebrate the successful establishment of the colony in New

Mexico, the settlers held a celebration to which they invited the chiefs of the surrounding Indian pueblos. A whole week was devoted to such spectacles as bullfights and cockfights. And to suitably impress their Indian guests, among whom were several spies come to gauge Spanish military strength, the settlers staged a drama which was destined to become a hallowed tradition in northern New Mexico. The play, performed in the open and complete with mock battle scenes, was entitled " Los Moros y los Cristianos" and re-enacted the 'Reconquista,' Spain's long struggle against the domination of the Moors. As the Spaniards intended, the Indians were particularly awed by the battle scenes with the dexterous display of horsemanship of the cavalry and the firepower of the infantry. As Villagra reports; "All this (the festivities) was concluded by a thunderous discharge of artillery, which caused great fear and wonder among the barbarians".

Soon after the settlement of San Gabriel, many of the colonists became disheartened at the prospects of taming the bleak land which would require massive irrigation projects to coax the desiccated earth to yield its fruits. Some of the younger adventurers felt that their newly acquired titles of nobility exempted them from the duty of manual labor. But, Onate, reacting to their complaints in the same way as John Smith was later to react in the Virginia colony, imposed a rule that one most work in order to eat. This policy angered many of his subjects and threats of mutiny and desertion soon became widespread.

Four disgruntled colonists actually attempted to carry out their threat. Abandoning the colony, they fled south to Mexico. As soon as Onate heard what had happened, he dispatched four of his captains to overtake the deserters and to execute them on the spot. It took the soldiers fourteen days to catch up with the fugitives and as Villagra, a member of the execution detail, relates: "Torquatus who ordered that his beloved son be beheaded for disobedience of orders, we had two of them executed. The other two escaped, abandoning their horses".

But this harsh example of the fate which awaited any would-be deserter did nothing to settle the discontent of Onate's colonists. Many had hoped that the mountains around San Gabriel, which resembled the hills of Zacatecas, would yield rich deposits of silver. Their disappointment was boundless when their initial surveys failed to turn up the expected rich veins of the precious metal.

Meanwhile, Onate, determined to make a success of his colony, sent out scouting parties to investigate the potential of the surrounding area for pastoral and agricultural pursuits. He was hopeful that the buffalo of the eastern plains could be domesticated, and to test his theory, he sent his nephew, Vicente de Zaldivar, with sixty men to reconnoiter the region. The group left in mid-September and returned on November 8th, 1598. Their reports discouraged any further efforts at taming the feral buffalo, which had proved too wild to be herded and had wounded several horses during the abortive attempts to corral them.

But another idea had captured the imagination of the Governor of

New Mexico: the discovery of the South Sea. Geographers had mistakenly placed these waters near New Mexico. Not only were they reputed to contain the fabled Pearl Fisheries which could make Onate fabulously wealthy, but they could provide a water route for the New Mexican settlers in their future trade with New Spain. Consequently, in October, 1598 Onate, leaving San Gabriel in charge of his other nephew, Juan de Zaldivar, with instructions to join him after the return of his brother from the eastern plains, set out in a southwesterly direction to discover the wealth of the 'Mar del Sur.'

But as he awaited the arrival of his nephew at his headquarters among the Zuni, the severest test yet of Spanish hegemony in New Mexico was about to be faced: the rebellion of the Acoma Pueblo. Juan de Zaldivar, with a small force of thirty men, had left San Gabriel to join Onate in his western explorations. On December 1, 1598, he reached the Acoma Pueblo which sits astride a high 'mesa,' 357 feet above the desert floor. According to Villagra, there were two factions among the Pueblo Indians, one in favor of friendly relations with the Spaniards, the other in favor of all-out warfare. The "evil genius" behind this latter group was the Acoman warrior, Zutacapan. As their leader, he promised the Indians that their liberties would be safeguarded and their lands freed from the presence of the rapacious Spaniards. A council of war was duly held at Acoma which approved of Zutacapan's plans for an uprising. Villagra disdainfully castigates the Acoman leader by comparing him to the devil: "A good example (of the lust for power) is this bloody savage, sprung from such ignoble forebears, and who like Lucifer, seeks to reach heights of power".

But Zaldivar and his soldiers were doomed when they bivouacked at the base of the Acoma 'mesa.' Ignorant of the hostile resolutions of the Indians, they climbed the steep trail, which consisted of nothing more than holes dug into the bare rock, and demanded food and blankets from the Indians. It was suggested to the Spanish that they send their men to the various houses where the hospitable villagers would satisfy their needs. The soldiers were ordered to disperse and to make the rounds of the different houses for provisions. But once the Spanish troops were scattered, the Indians struck with lightning speed. Vastly outnumbered, Zaldivar's men were no match for the superior Indian force and were quickly slaughtered. Only five survivors remained, fighting a rear-guard action all the way to the edge of the 'mesa' where one after the other, they leaped to the sand dunes below. Miraculously, four of their number survived and, joining the guards left in charge of the horses, hastened to warn their fellow colonists of this new turn of events, for they feared that the Acoma affair was the prelude to a general uprising of the Pueblo Indians. The survivors returned to San Gabriel to raise the alarm and to alert the friars in their isolated missions, while another group went in search of Onate to deliver the news of the ominous events which had taken place at Acoma.

A few weeks later, when all were assembled once again at San Gabriel, a solemn council was held which was both religious and military in nature. The religious question concerned the theological niceties of a "just war". Given the circumstances of the Acoma rebellion, the theologians were asked if there existed sufficient cause to retaliate against the rebel pueblo. Fray Alonso Martinez, an able theologian, delivered a lengthy dissertation to the Governor expounding on the doctrinal principles which governed a "just war." Essentially, Fray Martinez reiterated medieval Catholic dogma, namely, that a war was justified to "punish those who are guilty of wrongdoing, or who have violated the laws of the land".

After all the priests had signed the theological opinion, Villagra reports that the Governor's conscience was set at ease and he ordered that "war by blood and fire be proclaimed against the Indians of Acoma". Seventy soldiers were chosen to take part in the punitive expedition against the Acomans. Vicente de Zaldivar, whose brother Juan had been slain in the Acoma uprising, was given the commission to lead the Spanish forces. Before they departed from San Gabriel, the soldiers confessed their sins to the Franciscan friars and received the sacrament of the Eucharist, for it was the devout belief of the Spaniards that no Christian soldier should venture into battle unconfessed and unrepentant; to do so, would incure the risk of eternal damnation should he fall in combat. And so, all were duly shriven except one hapless individual who chose to flaunt this pious practice, and later, according to Villagra, reaped his just desserts when he was accidentally killed by a companion during the assault on Acoma. But "all's well that ends well", and "this abandoned wretch, in spite of his many wounds made his way to the tent of the priest, where, having confessed his sins, he breathed his last".

The Spanish soldiers, eager for revenge, descended upon the Acoma pueblo. Determined to make the Indians pay dearly for their audacity in challenging their rule, the Spaniards waged a no-quarter campaign against the enemy. In retrospect, their conduct of the battle and its aftermath seems unusually cruel even for the callous Spanish who were inured to the primitive cruelty of medieval warfare. But they were determined to teach the Indians of New Mexico a salutary lesson calculated to impress on them the futility of rebellion.

The 70-man expedition arrived at Acoma on January 21, 1599, armed with two cannons and an assortment of war materiel. In accordance with accepted custom, a captain read the "requerimiento" in solemn tones, informing the Indians that they could immediately submit to Spanish authority and accept the judicial consequences of their rebellion. In reply, Zutucapan and his warriors jeered at the Spaniards from the heights of their impregnable fortress and reinforced their disdain by hurling rocks from atop the 'mesa.' But the Spanish officers were veteran campaigners and their troops were hardened combat soldiers, skilled in the tactics of European siege warfare. Zaldivar put into operation a plan often used in breaching the defenses of European walled cities and medieval fortresses. As a diversionary tactic, he threw the bulk of his forces against the main approach to the 'mesa' where he knew the Indians expected the assault to take place. Meanwhile, twelve of his men secretly scaled the rocks at the far end of the 'mesa' using grappling hooks and ropes to climb to the top. They were even successful in hauling one of the artillery pieces to the summit and placing it in advantageous position. However, the commandos were soon discovered by the Acomans and were forced to fight a long and bloody battle.

The Indians were led by Gicombo, one of their chieftains. But the superior fire-power of the enemy, coupled with their "just wrath", eventually threw the advantage to the Spanish invaders. Villagra reports how the sight of one of the enemy dressed in the clothes of a slaughtered Spaniard aroused the fighting spirit of the troops to fever pitch: "The sergeant major, seeing a savage impudently arrayed in the garments of his murdered brother, leaped upon the savage and with one blow cleft his skull asunder, leaving the miserable wretch bathed in his gore and his brother's garments transformed into a bloody funeral shroud".

Successfully engaging the Acomans on two fronts, the Spaniards were able to repulse the Indians' counter-attack and gain the top of the 'mesa.' On the following morning, the main body of troops bridged the chasm which divided the 'mesa' into two sections and attacked the villagers with musket and cannon, setting fire to the pueblo and slaughtering men, women and children. The Indians suffered heavy losses which, before the end of the three-day battle, exceeded 600 dead and hundreds more wounded. Stubbornly, the Acomans refused the exhortations of the Spaniards to surrender and many of them, rather than be taken prisoner, hurled themselves from the top of the 'mesa' onto the rocks below or into the burning houses; some hanged themselves from tree limbs, while others even "turned their arms against each other...father slew son, and son slew father."

The fight continued from house to house amidst the fires, the noise and the confusion. Villagra reports that so disoriented was the general tenor of the fighting that "Asencio de Archuleta, in the excitement, lifted his harquebus and, without noticing where he shot, sent four bullets through the body of his most trusted friend".

In the end, superior military technology decided the outcome of the battle. Although there was no lack of bravery and even fanaticism on both sides, it was the introduction of the two artillery pieces which spelled the difference between victory and defeat. The two cannons were maneuvered into position, loaded with four hundred iron balls and fired at point-blank range into a dense crowd of three hundred Indians. The resultant carnage was frightful. As Villagra reports: "When the smoke clears one can see some seeking safety in flight, others upon the ground, some dragging a broken wing, some dragging their entrails in the dust...It was a gruesome and terrible sight".

At last, when the Indian leaders had either been killed or had committed suicide, the elders of the tribe called a halt to the butchery of their people and surrendered. The Spanish victory against overwhelming odds was indeed an occasion for rejoicing. It was also reason to thank the Christian saints for their intervention. Many an imaginative Spaniard swore he had seen Santiago, patron of warriors, riding his white charger in the sky above the Spanish forces, a sure sign of victory. Other equally pious troopers attributed their victory to the intercession of the Blessed Virgin.

But flagrant rebellion could not go unpunished, and Onate brought the Acoma Indians to trial. With strict regard for the legalistic niceties of Spanish justice, he appointed a court defender, Alonso Gomez Montesinos, to represent the interests of the Acomans. Of course, this apparent gesture of impartiality was a mere formality, since Indian guilt was already predetermined. As Governor, Onate presided at the trial which consisted mostly of accusations by Spanish soldiers regarding the perfidy of the Acoma Indians. The latter were judged guilty as charged and on February 12, 1599, sentence was passed on the unfortunate survivors of the sanguinary affair. Not surprisingly, the full rigor of medieval law, as interpreted by Onate and his advisors, was enforced against the unfortunate Acomans. The judicial sentence condemned all males over the age of 25 to have one foot cut off and to pledge themselves to 25 years of personal service to their Spanish overlords. Young men between 12 and 25 years of age were spared this mutilation, but had to devote 25 years of servitude, while females over the age of twelve were condemned to 20 years of slavery. The transcripts of the trial also mention the fact that 60 of the surviving young women were sent to Mexico city for distribution among the various convents of womens' religious orders.

The severity of the Spanish sentence against the Acoma Indians cannot be judged fairly by today's more humane standards of punitive justice; happily, yesterday's legalized barbarisms have given way to a more benign system of criminal law. But, of course, the Spaniards were pragmatic conquerors, and their ruthlessness had the desired effect. Immediately after the Acoma insurrection, the other pueblos renewed their allegiance to the Crown of Spain. The major result of the trial and its aftermath was the effective curtailment of incipient rebellion among the Indians, although revolutionary sentiment would continue to simmer below the surface for more than 70 years until it burst forth in the Pueblo Revolt of 1680. After the decisive subjugation of the Acoma Indians, plans for further explorations were high on Onate's agenda. In 1600, he dispatched Vicente Zaldivar to search for the shores of the Pacific Ocean, but there is no record of the success or failure of this mission. Another of the Governor's priorities was the need for reinforcements for his struggling colony. On March 2, 1599, he drafted a letter to the Viceroy, which lauded the potential of New Mexico as an agricultural and pastoral center capable of producing revenues for the Spanish Crown. He also requested a fresh contingent of colonists to stimulate the development of the territory. Doubtlessly, Onate's pleas were instrumental in the Viceroy's decision to bolster the settlement at San Gabriel with new recruits chosen from among the restive inhabitants of New Spain. In response to Onate's request, 73 soldiers and eight Franciscan missionaries embarked on the long journey northward, arriving in San Gabriel on Christmas Eve, 1600.

With the infusion of new blood into his colony, Onate decided that the time was ripe to launch an exploratory trip to the eastern plains in search of the Gran Ouivira. In June, 1601, he set out with a force of approximately 80 men, 6 wagons, and 700 head of livestock. They encountered some peaceful Apache Indians along the way and it is reported that the Spanish marvelled at the Indian custom of using large domesticated dogs as beasts of burden. But their contacts with other Plains Indians were less fortuitous. The Osage of Kansas stubbornly resisted Spanish overtures of friendship and engaged Onate's men in a running battle. The Spaniards were no match for these fleet-footed adversaries and soon deemed it expedient to abandon their quest for Quivira and return to the comparative safety of San Gabriel.

Thus, Onate's odessey on the eastern plains produced no more positive results than that of Coronado eighty years earlier. When the Governor returned to San Gabriel in November, 1601, he found the settlement all but abandoned, for the majority of the colonists had fled to Mexico, leaving only twenty-five of the original inhabitants. The reason for their hasty departure during Onate's absence was not hard to fathom. Many of the settlers had become bitterly disillusioned at the barren, inhospitable terrain of their new home and the meager prospects for prosperity which it offered. And they complained of the repressive demands of their leader which only exacerbated their discontent. In their efforts to defect, they were abetted by the Franciscan friars who deplored the brutality of the Governor toward the conquered Acoma Indians. Their consciences were bothered not so much by the enforcement of medieval justice, but by the fact that such harshness had the effect of negating their missionary activities among the resentful populace of the territory. Not surprisingly, the preachment of Christian love and compassion seemed utterly paradoxical in the face of the atrocities committed in the name of the Catholic King. Consequently, Spanish Catholicism was hard pressed to maintain its credibility among the Pueblo Indians throughout these years and, indeed, for most of the seventeenth century.

On learning of the wholesale abandonment of his colony, Onate first called to account his deputy, the Lieutenant-Governor, Francisco de Sosa Penalosa, and the religious superior, Padre Juan de Escalona. Both men expressed their inability to alter the determination of the colonists who were unwilling to continue to face the hazards of a precarious existence on the frontier.

For Onate, the desertion of his subjects spelled disaster. He rightfully suspected that the very worst reports of his conduct and administration would be conveyed to the Viceroy by his disgruntled subjects. Determined to rally the colonists and persuade them to return to New Mexico, he dispatched an emissary, armed with an official pardon, to overtake the deserters and persuade them to return to San Gabriel. But his belated attempt to avert disaster was unsuccessful, for the bulk of the colonists had already reached Mexico and placed themselves under the protection of the Viceroy. He, in turn, gave credence to their negative reports and issued an official order stating that the settlers could not be forced to return to the northern frontier.

Onate received the news with foreboding, knowing that the decision meant that both the Viceroy and the government's judicial branch, the 'Audiencia,' were seriously considering abandoning the whole enterprise in New Mexico. If this were to be their decision, it was but a short step for the King and the Council of the Indies to withdraw all support for the fledgling colony. He decided to make a last-chance effort to salvage both his colony and his reputation by leading a small expedition of 30 soldiers in search of the wealth of the Pearl Fisheries.

A brief record of this treasure hunt was etched into a rock at El Morro in southwestern New Mexico with the words: "Paso por aqui el adelantado Don Juan de Onate del descubrimiento de la Mar del sur a 16 de April de 1605." (The 'adelantado,' Don Juan de Onate, passed this way after his discovery of the South Sea on April 16, 1605.) These words were inscribed on the rock over an ancient Indian pictograph by a member of Onate's exploring party on its return journey from the Gulf of California. But, as on so many occasions, Spanish hopes for easy riches were once again frustrated upon their arrival at the Southern Sea. Firstly, the Pearl Fisheries were obviously a myth; secondly, the sea (Gulf of California) was too far away from the populated area of New Mexico to function as a viable trade route to Mexico.

In desperation, Onate sent his nephew, Vicente de Zaldivar, to the Spanish court to plead his cause. But the Council of the Indies ignored Zaldivar's advocacy and directed the new Viceroy, the Marquis de Montesclaros, to make a recommendation on the case. In his report, Montesclaros faulted the whole New Mexico venture as a wasteful expenditure of human and material resources. He advised the Council to continue the settlement solely for missionary purposes and to forbid further useless explorations for mineral wealth which appeared to be non-existant.

The Council took the advice of Montesclaros, especially his recommendation to replace Onate as Governor with a more reliable and prudent individual. Onate, himself, seeing the writing on the wall, tendered his resignation to the Viceroy who immediately accepted it and appointed an interim Governor to oversee the rehabilitation of the colony. Since the latter was a former subordinate, it must have been particularly galling for Onate to comply with the Viceroy's command to remain in New Mexico under the acting Governor until some disposition of his case could be made.

The fact that Onate had not achieved the success of a Pizarro or a Cortez in discovering the riches of the Aztec and Inca empires for Spain definitively sealed his fate. When his case finally came before the 'Audiencia,' the judicial arm of government in Mexico City, he was formally accused of thirty charges of mismanagement of the colony and mistreatment of the Indians. His case came to trial in 1614 and he was found guilty of twelve major crimes. Besides the indictments alleging ill treatment of the Indians of Acoma, an accusation of sexual misconduct was thrown in for good measure. In view of the tenor of the times and the severity of his transgressions, Onate's sentence was fairly light: he was banished for ever from New Mexico; he was not permitted to enter Mexico City for four years and he was stripped of the prestigious titles of Governor, Captain-General and 'Adelantado.' In addition, he was fined six thousands ducats, a heavy financial burden for Onate who had already spent the greater part of the family fortune in attempting to colonize New Mexico. For many years afterward, Onate fought the verdict at the Royal Court in Spain until his persistence was finally rewarded, when King Philip IV reversed the decision of the 'Audiencia' and restored his titles and his good name. Subsequently, he was appointed royal inspector for the mines in Spain and died in obscurity in 1627 at Guadalcanal, a small town located thirty miles north of Sevilla.

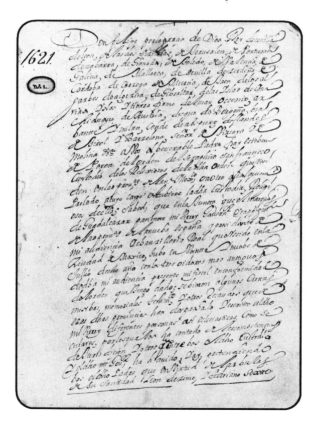

Figure 5: Royal directive to Fray Esteban de Perea, Custodian of the Franciscans in New Mexico. Spanish Archives of New Mexico 11. No. 1. New Mexico State Records Center and Archives.

CHAPTER 5

THE SETTLEMENT

The fact that the Council of the Indies did not entirely abandon all further attempts to colonize New Mexico attests to the habitual pietism underlying many political decisions of the Spanish Crown whose foreign policy had to deal with the future of thousands of Indian converts to Catholicism. The neophytes were decidedly too numerous to transfer 'en masse' to Mexico, and so to aid the policy makers in finding a solution favoring the continued presence of the Spanish government in New Mexico, the Franciscan missionaries provided highly inflated statistics, claiming to have baptized between 9,000 and 10,000 souls. As a consequence, the decision was made to declare New Mexico a royal colony and to develop the region for purposes of evangelization.

Meanwhile, a new Governor, Pedro de Peralta, had been appointed in 1609. Arriving in San Gabriel in the winter of that year, he decided with the consent of the Viceroy to relocate the capital of the colony further down river since San Gabriel was now considered unsuited for defense purposes, for it was situated too close to the Tewa pueblos. It is possible that Onate may have anticipated this decision during his tenure in office and founded a small settlement at a location at the southern end of a spur of the Rockies (later named the Sangre de Cristo Mountains).

Chosen for its defense potential, the Spaniards named their new "Villa", Santa Fe, after the town of the same name which had been built by Queen Isabella outside the Moorish stronghold of Granada during the final stages of the "Reconquista". Very likely the Spanish saw a parallel between their former crusade against the infidel Moors and their present struggle against the heathen Indians; both conflicts represented the triumph of the "Santa Fe" (Holy Faith) over the Forces of Darkness. Hence, their new capital should bear a name epitomizing the intensity of the Faith with which the Spanish approached the conquest.

Firstly, a 'plaza' was built under the system of "repartimiento" by which Indians were conscripted to serve as a labor force. Municipal land grants were parceled out among the colonists and grazing and farm lands were assigned according to the accepted custom and regulations governing the distribution of lands in a new area. The "Casa Real" (now referred to as the Palace of the Governors) was built at the edge of the 'plaza', where the

prominent figures in the colonial administration had their offices.
Along with the civil government, the Catholic Church also established itself firmly in New Mexico to continue its missionary work. The head of the Franciscan friars, the custodian, established his headquarters at the Queres pueblo of Santo Domingo. From this ecclesiastical center, the missionary programs of the Catholic Church were administered at considerable cost to the secular government. During the next 70 years, it is estimated that the evangelization of the Indians cost the Spanish Crown a million pesos, a large sum of money for that time. But unfortunately, the work of conversion and pacification was marred during the seventeenth century by an acrimonious conflict between the Church and State. As France V. Scholes, an expert on seventeenth century New Mexico, expressed it in the title of his scholarly treatise, these were "Troublous Times in New Mexico".

Besides the missionary motive, Spain's decision to settle New Mexico was also pragmatic. Already France, England and the Netherlands were challenging Iberian claims in the western hemisphere. Fear of foreign intrusion prompted the Spanish authorities to secure their northern borders by garrisoning New Mexico, thereby laying unconditional claim to the vast northern frontier. Yet, in the hierarchy of motives, the major impetus for colonizing the region sprang from zeal for evangelization.

When they first arrived in the New World, the Spanish conquistadors were horrified by the idolatry of the Aztecs expressed in the ritual of human sacrifice. Medieval Scholasticism had condemned such practices as devil-inspired and therefore, it was commonly believed that the Indians were children of Satan. Fortunately for the Franciscans, no such aberrant practices existed in New Mexico and the friars were confident that a fertile field of missionary activity awaited them. From its headquarters at Santo Domingo, the Church began the systematic conversion of the Pueblo Indians whose religious practices were considered to be expressions of primitive animism, easily susceptible to the blandishments of Christianity. Thus, the Church's first mistake was its inability to appreciate the underlying cosmology and religious world-view of a people whose sedentary corn culture had long since afforded them the luxury of creating a sophisticated mythology. The fact that the simple Spanish mendicant friars underestimated the force of the native beliefs would cost them dearly in the long run.

The Church's error in failing to correctly assess the psychological adherence of Indian tribes to their various religions was further compounded by its obstinate refusal to cooperate with the secular authorities in the business of evangelization. Although the papacy had granted the "Patronato Real" to the Spanish crown in the Bull "Inter Caetera," by which the secular powers were given jurisdiction in Church affairs, the Catholic Church in New Mexico was constantly at loggerheads with the civil authorities over control of the Indians. In spite of the legal strictures governing any autonomous action by the Church, the Franciscans ignored the intent of the 'Patronato' and unilaterally continued to carry out their basic mandate to forge ahead with the task of conversion.

The State, on the other hand, paid only lip service to the missionary purposes of the royal colony of New Mexico. In the New World, the Indians represented a potential work force which the State intended to exploit to the fullest. Horrendous examples of such exploitation had already manifested themselves in the Caribbean Islands where the Indian population had been decimated within a generation after the discovery of the region.

Essentially, the Church-State conflict took the form of an acrid debate over their respective rights with regard to the Indian. Faced with the State's penchant to exploit the latter, the Church posed as the protector of the Indians. However, the civil authorities routinely accused the Catholic establishment of furthering its own ends by rounding up large numbers of Indians in mission complexes under the guise of conversion, but, in reality, using Indian manpower to create an ecclesiastical mini-empire in New Mexico.

With the advantage of hindsight, it is not difficult to analyze the motives of the respective powers in their treatment of the Indian. Certainly in utilizing an indigenous population as a labor supply, the Church pursued its mission as a spiritual entity, yet one with temporal needs in the form of land, buildings and the means of subsistence. As for the secular authorities, the dictates of the laws of "encomienda" and "repartimiento" allowed them to view the native population as a labor market to be exploited to the utmost. Either way, it was the Indian, caught in the middle of a rapacious competition for his services, who suffered at the hands of both Church and State during the seventeenth century.

The Spanish poet, Lope De Vega, scathingly referred to the Church's motivations for evangelization in his play "El Nuevo Mundo": "It is not Christianity that leads them on, but rather gold and greed." Few historians would entirely agree with his cynical statement that Christianization was merely a hypocritical justification for exploitation. Yet, 'de facto,' both the Church and State exploited the Indian in seventeenth-century New Mexico and fought bitterly over the spoils.

It is difficult for us in the twentieth century to fully comprehend the acrimony of the Church-State conflict. The overall animosity of one toward the other is best appreciated by examining the controversy at the personal level, where the clash of personalities demonstrated the underlying resentment of the clergy toward government officials and 'vice versa.'

Bitter quarreling broke out as early as 1610, under the governorship of Peralta. From that point on, it grew in intensity so that by 1650 virtual civil war between Church and State threatened the peace of the colony. The extent of the conflict varied depending on the character of the Governor and the current head of the Franciscan Order. In 1610, Peralta felt compelled by the exigencies of his building program to draw heavily on the Indian labor force, a policy which resulted in a head-on collision with Church authorities.

In 1612, Fray Isidro Ordonez arrived in New Mexico to take charge of the missions. Although many Franciscans were zealous and dedicated missionaries, competing spiritual and material goals were inevitably present in their single-minded efforts to convert the Indian. In the case of Ordonez, spiritual concerns seem to have been obscured by material objectives. An arrogant, intolerant, and cantankerous individual, he claimed ecclesiastical jurisdiction over New Mexico, asserting that he was an agent of the Inquisition. In this capacity, he demanded instant obedience from both the missionaries and the secular authorities. He was so universally hated that even one of his own friars intimated to the Governor that Ordonez' credentials of office were probably forgeries. Peralta demanded to see his papers, but Ordonez refused to show them, thus lending credence to the accusation. Ordonez countered the charge by officially accusing the Governor of exploiting the Indians and threatened him with excommunication, the most effective weapon in the Church's spiritual arsenal. In fact, added Ordonez, anyone attempting to defend the position of Peralta was subject to 'ipso facto' excommunication.

As relations between Church and State continued to deteriorate, Ordonez constantly meddled in civil matters and heaped abuse upon the Governor. Verbal insults flew back and forth between Santa Fe and Santo Domingo, and soon violence broke out over an attempt by Ordonez to countermand some orders issued by the Governor. In May, 1613, a detachment of troops was sent to Taos by Governor Peralta. Ordonez encountered the soldiers 'en route' at Nambe Pueblo and promptly ordered them back to Santa Fe to attend Holy Mass, since it was the Feast of Pentecost. When they arrived at the capital, the Governor ordered them back to Taos with instructions to attend Mass at one of the pueblos along the way. Ordonez, on being told of the Governor's action, became extremely incensed at Peralta's temerity in countermanding his orders and, in retaliation, summarily excommunicated him.

A decree of excommunication was a powerful medieval device used with telling effect by the Church to keep the erring laity in line. Officially, it cut off the individual Catholic from all communion with his fellow Christians and forbade him to receive the sacraments. Unless the strictures were lifted, it was tantamount to a decree of damnation, for if a person should die in such a state, his eternal doom was sealed. However, what angered the Governor more than the excommunication, was the discovery that his favorite chair in the Santa Fe parish church had been unceremoniously thrown into a mud puddle in the central 'plaza.' Convinced that this was the work of Ordonez, the Governor confronted the friar and in a paroxism of anger, drew his pistol and fired at him. In true comic-opera style, the bullet missed Ordonez, striking and wounding two onlookers. Perhaps Peralta was somewhat mollified when he discovered that one of those wounded was a cleric. Ordonez continued to denounce the Governor from the pulpit, insulting him with the worst seventeenth-century expletives which came to mind. His most serious charge accused the Governor of being a "heretic Lutheran".

Finally, Peralta decided to go to Mexico City and lay the whole matter before the Viceroy. He set out from Santa Fe with a small detachment of soldiers, but was stopped by Ordonez near the Isleta Pueblo. In the name of the Holy Inquisition, the Governor was arrested and placed in jail at the Sandia mission, leaving Ordonez 'de facto' ruler of New Mexico.

After suffering the confinement of an ecclesiastical jail for some time, Peralta managed to smuggle out a letter to the Viceroy in Mexico City. In 1614, a new Governor was sent to the territory with orders to recall both Peralta and Ordonez. Subsequently, the former Governor was exonerated of all charges brought against him by the friar; for his part, Ordonez was disciplined and confined to a monastary of the Franciscan Order for falsely claiming to be a representative of the Inquisition.

CHAPTER 6

THE REBELLION

As early as the 1630s, small-scale Indian uprisings had begun to take place in protest against Spanish rule. In the year 1632, a disturbance broke out in the Zuni Pueblo of Hawikuh. On a Sunday morning in February, the parishioners entered the church as usual to attend Mass and listen to the sermon of their pastor, Fray Francisco de Letrado. At a given signal, a group of warriors fired a volley of arrows at the friar as he celebrated the Mass; as he lay dying, they scalped him. When the news of the priest's murder reached Santa Fe, the Governor dispatched a contingent of troops to subdue the Zunis. The perpetrators of the crime sought refuge on Corn Mountain, their sacred 'mesa,' but, upon the promise of a full pardon, they submitted to the Spanish captain and docilely returned to the fold.

In the following year, a Franciscan priest ministering to the spiritual needs of the Hopis was murdered by his parishioners and, in that same year, the people of Jemez revolted and assassinated their parish priest. In Taos in 1639, the Indians murdered their pastor and destroyed the church. But the major conspiracy which constituted the forerunner of subsequent catastrophic events, took place in the late 1640s. The 'cacique' of the Tompiro Indians created a loose union of neighboring pueblos whose avowed purpose was rebellion against the Spanish. However, their plot was discovered and eight of the ring leaders were executed.

Although the remote causes of the Pueblo Revolt embodied in the foregoing accounts were mainly religious in nature, there also existed some immediate causes which exacerbated the explosive situation and ignited the incipient spark of rebellion which eventually grew into a full-blown conflagration. During the 17th century, the Spaniards exploited Indian laborers as part of the policy of both Church and State, forcing them to work under extremely harsh conditions in 'obrajes' (sweat shops) weaving "mantas" (blankets) to be used in trade with the provinces of New Spain. They were also employed in collecting salt and pinon nuts and in hunting the buffalo for their hides. Almost exclusively, the profits from these economic ventures found their way into the pockets of the various Governors, who considered the acquisition of such ill-gotten gains as part of the perquisites of office. The Church, too, demanded its share of Indian labor to help build the vast complex of missions, farms, churches and convents throughout New Mexico. Indians undertook the agricultural work and cared for the herds of livestock which the missionaries kept for trading purposes. But, after dividing their labor between Church and State, there was very little left for the Indians to fulfill their own needs, and it was the growing discontent with this state of affairs which nourished the germ of rebellion among them.

Another factor which helped to account for the major Revolt in 1680 was superstition, generated by a series of natural disasters. In a corn culture, water is essential to life; in its absence, the fields dry up and the crops wither. Between 1650 and 1680 New Mexico suffered several protracted dry spells which caused widespread famine in the pueblos. During the drought-ridden years, between 1668 and 1672, it is reported that as many as 500 Indians died yearly. These natural phenomena were interpreted by the Indians as the adverse judgment of their gods against the white man's religion, which had led them to abandon the traditional rain-making ceremonies, causing the gods to withhold the saving rain-waters.

Thus, the smoldering antagonism toward the totality of Spanish rule in 17th century New Mexico came into sharp focus, reinforced by the drought which the shamans interpreted as a direct signal from the gods to return to the old ways. The Revolt of 1680 would be a desperate attempt to appease the angry gods of the pueblos and return to the pristine worship of the ancestral deities. The resultant rebellion would not have been a success without the guiding genius of a dynamic personality, the Indian Pope, a medicine-man from the San Juan Pueblo. It was his ability to unite disparate groups of Indians in a common cause and to outmaneuver the Spaniards, using their own tactics against them, that enabled the Indians of New Mexico to engineer one of the greatest defeats Spain had thus far suffered in the New World.

By the year 1650, the Church-State conflict had escalated to the point where civil war was imminent. Incidents such as the forcible expulsion from Santa Fe of a group of friars by soldiers of the overnor and the stockpiling of weapons at the Santa Domingo mission, underscored the fundamental differences dividing the secular and ecclesiastical authorities. But serious as was the hatred between these two Spanish institutions, it was nothing compared to the bitterness which marked the relationship between missionaries and Indians.

At first the process of evangelization had progressed smoothly. Thousands of Indians had been initiated into the Catholic Church through the sacrament of Baptism. They accepted the tenets of the Christian Faith and, in varying degrees of conformity, observed the commandments of the Church regarding the mandatory observance of the Catholic Liturgy. Yet the adult Indian tended to withhold his inner, psychological allegiance from these foreign beliefs. Although he could identify somewhat with Catholicism's "cultus duliae", devotion to the Saints, recognizing many parallels between the role of the saints and that of the gods in his own pantheon, he nevertheless continued to observe the age-old rituals and to cling to his ancestral beliefs in spite of his outward obeisance to the religion of the friars. Most scholars conclude that the "conversion" of the Pueblo Indians to Catholicism was merely the acceptance of the outer husk of Christianity. In reality, the superimposition upon an indigenous culture of a complicated theological system, which was little understood by the natives of New Mexico, served only to alienate the reluctant neophytes, whose outward observance belied their inward rejection of the Spaniards' religion. And, as this paradox between outward conformity and inward rebellion to Christianity became increasingly obvious to the friars, they began to prohibit Indian dances and other ceremonies which had religious overtones. By 1630, it was apparent that the Indians had not given up their secret religious ceremonies; masked kachina dances were still held regularly; prayer ceremonies in the kivas were an everyday feature of village life and corn meal was still strewn ritually. To add insult to injury, the clergy realized that some Governors, in particular Lopez de Mendizabal, permitted native rituals as part of the welcoming ceremonies during their visits to the pueblos. The missionaries interpreted such leniency as the condoning of heresy, and they complained bitterly to the Viceroy about the Governor's penchant for pagan rituals.

Before the administration of Governor Lopez de Mendizabal, the friars had taken limited steps to suppress Indian ceremonials. However, as a direct result of the "laxity" of the Governor, who considered such ceremonies as mere "Indian foolishness," the Franciscan custodian in 1661, decreed an absolute prohibition on kachina dances, solemnly instructing the friars to confiscate all materials of "idolatry," in particular the kachina masks. Within a few months, numerous kivas were systematically ransacked and about 1600 masks were confiscated and publicly burned in the village 'plazas.' An appeal was made by the Governor to the "Audiencia" in Mexico City on behalf of the Indians. Surprisingly, the courts denounced the search-and-destroy mission of the Franciscans, stating that the burden of proof regarding the superstitious character of the kachina dances lay with the missionaries. So far, claimed the "Audiencia", the friars had failed to furnish such proof; therefore, the Governor was perfectly within his rights in permitting the public performance of the dances. But these directives from Mexico City seem to have been ignored by the missionaries in New Mexico, and, later, under Governor Juan Francisco Trevino, the civil authorities actively aided the friars in their campaign to erradicate the native religions. Those Indians caught in the act of practicing their religion were accused of witchcraft and idolatry and handed over to the secular arm of the law for punishment. Besides burning the trappings of the Indian religious rituals, these punishments often took the form of public floggings at the whipping post and, as an extreme humiliation, the shaving of the heads of "apostate and wayward Indians". The overall failure of these measures would soon become apparent in 1680 when the Pueblo Indians rose up in a body against their Spanish overlords and mercilessly drove them out of all the lands of New Mexico.

On the morning of August 10, 1680, Governor Antonio de Otermin received the ominous news that Padre Juan Bautista, pastor of the Tesuque Pueblo, had been murdered, his livestock stolen and his church desecrated. Although unaware of the full gravity of the situation, the Governor had already received advance warning of the projected Indian uprising from two Tano Indians, who had reported to him on the previous day. He immediately dispatched a troop of soldiers to ascertain the extent of the damage at Tesuque. But he was not prepared for the horrifying news which the frightened troopers brought back from the pueblo. The whole of northern New Mexico, they reported, was in flames; priests, religious brothers, men, women and children had been brutally murdered and their dwelling places put to the torch. These horror stories were confirmed as the survivors of the massacre in the North began to straggle into Santa Fe with stories of the atrocities they had witnessed and blessedly escaped.

The revolt was the result of a Pan-Indian movement which had developed under the aegis of Pope, whose sole purpose was to end the Spanish domination of his ancestral lands. Originally, the date for the rebellion had been set for August 13, and knotted cords had been distributed to the confederated pueblos to serve as primitive calendars to count the days till D-Day. However, when Pope found out about the betrayal of his plans on August 9, he ordered hostilities to commence immediately. So efficient was his communications' network that within a day, the pueblos rose up in a body against their Spanish oppressors. Symptomatic of their hatred for the white man's religion was the fact that they struck first at the churches, murdering the priests and profaning the altars. Of the 33 missionaries then working in northern New Mexico, 21 were killed in the initial surprise attacks.

As the revolt gained momentum, settlers from the ranches and farms of the area continued to pour into Santa Fe ahead of the Indians. In an attempt to garrison the city, the Governor quartered the refugees in government buildings and ordered everyone to congregate within the fortified sector of the 'plaza' area. Arms were then distributed to all the able-bodied men, and the women were assigned to store food and water in preparation for the expected siege.

On the morning of August 13, the advance columns of Indians began to arrive, infiltrating the southern suburbs of the town and taking up key positions near the fortified 'plaza.' The mix of tribes intent on the destruction of the Spanish was awesome. Besides the warriors of the northern pueblos, the Indian squadrons consisted of Tanos, Pecos, Keres, Tewas and Jemez Indians. To his dismay, the Governor also learned that the traditional enemies of the pueblos, the Apaches, had temporarily submerged their differences and joined the rebellion.

Hoping for a reprieve for his beleaguered garrision, the Governor arranged to parley with the Indians. A Tano chieftan, a former friend of the Spanish, came forward to bargain with the Governor. He carried with him two wooden crosses and offered Otermin the alternative of choosing a red cross, symbol of war, or a white cross, symbol of peace. If the Governor were to choose the former, the chief threatened that the colonists would be annihilated; but if he chose the latter, they would be permitted to leave the city and the province unmolested.

Realizing that the Indians were stalling for time while reinforcements arrived, Otermin ignored the ultimatum and, seizing the initiative, crossed the Santa Fe River with a small force and attacked the Indians in the Barrio de Analco on the outskirts of the town. But the rebels repelled the attack and forced the Spanish to retreat to their fortified 'plaza.'

Meanwhile, the 13th, and 14th, of August, saw hundreds of Indians arriving from the most distant pueblos and from the great plains in the East. They completely surrounded the city, encamping in the foothills where the glow of their campfires illumined the night sky, striking fear into the Spanish survivors huddled in the royal buildings in the town center. With a pitiful force of 150 fighting men, they were vastly outnumbered by more than two thousand Indian warriors; nevertheless, they gallantly prepared for the inevitable mass attack on Santa Fe and prayed to St. James for victory in the name of the Holy Faith.

At last, on August 16th, 1680, the dreaded attack on Santa Fe took place. Wave upon wave of Indian warriors stormed the inner fortifications only to be repelled by the Spanish defenders. But the overwhelming numerical superiority of the attackers was bound to make itself felt in the end. By nightfall, Indian forces had breached the outer defenses and were pressing against the perimeter around the Palace of the Governors. Pope, the Indian leader, had devised a strategy calculated to bring the defenders to their knees: he cut off the main water supply by damning the "acequia madre" which carried water from the river to the town center.

The night of August 16th was decisive for the besieged Spanish garrison. Faced with the alternative of either retreating southwards or standing up to his adversaries, Otermin decided to defy his enemies and engage them in a last-ditch stand. Accordingly, on the following morning, the Governor sallied forth at the head of his remaining troops and engaged the Indian warriors in a fiercely contested battle which lasted most of the day. In the vanguard of the fray the Governor himself, his face and chest covered with blood from three arrow wounds, maneuvered his cavalry to advantage so that his troops were able to overcome the forward enemy positions, killing 300 Indians and capturing 47, who were later interrogated and executed by firing squad in the Santa Fe 'plaza.'

The ferocity of the Spanish attack had taken the Indians by surprise. Some troops had even managed to reach the bank of the river and to bring back water to their compatriots in the palace fortifications. But in spite of these minor successes, Otermin realized the situation was hopeless, and he made the decision to retreat down river to attempt to link up with the remnants of those colonists who had taken refuge with the Lieutenant-Governor, Alonso Garcia, in the Isleta Pueblo. But Garcia, convinced that his group of 1500 colonists were the only survivors of the great revolt, had left the pueblo and begun a strategic retreat southwards.

Meanwhile in Santa Fe, Otermin led his bedraggled survivors out of the fortified 'plaza,' forming a column with women and children in the center surrounded by his troops. In fear and trepidation, the formation inched forward under the watchful eyes of hundreds of Indian warriors, who, however, did not give battle, perhaps realizing that the foreigners were leaving their territory forever and that it would be self-defeating to engage them in another bloody fight.

Unmolested, the survivors arrived at the Isleta Pueblo in the first days of September, 1680. When Otermin learned that the Lieutenant-Governor had already left for the South, apparently leaving him to his fate, he was angry and sent a messenger after Garcia with news of what had taken place in the North and with orders to return immediately. The initial angry confrontation between Otermin and Garcia was quickly tempered when the latter explained that he had acted in the best interests of the refugees congregated at Isleta. News had reached him that the whole northern sector had been laid waste and that there were no survivors. Otermin accepted his deputy's explanation, and both groups joined forces and proceeded together down river to the El Paso region.

When he arrived, the governor took stock of the situation in his report to the Viceroy in Mexico City, presenting him with an 'apologia' for his role in the abysmal defeat of Spanish arms. In an effort to exonerate himself, Otermin painted a less dismal picture of the revolt, offering excuses for his lack of foresight in not anticipating the rebellion and lowering the number of Spanish deaths to a mere 400, although historians agree that there were as many as 1000 victims of the slaughter in New Mexico. In his response, the Viceroy ordered Otermin to hold his colony together and to make immediate plans for the reconquest of the northern regions. El Paso was designated interim capital of the Kingdom of New Mexico and would enjoy that distinction for the next twelve years.

During their years of exile in El Paso, the New Mexican colonists reorganized the 'cabildo,' (the town council) and laid plans for the eventual reconquest of the province. However, many of the refugees were discouraged at the ruination of their lands and property, and they despaired of ever rebuilding their lost fortunes in New Mexico. For them, the El Paso region offered a secure haven and they were content to remain there, far from the bellicose pueblos in the North.

Meanwhile Otermin selected a few battle-hardened troops, and in an attempt to vindicate himself in the eyes of the Viceroy and regain his lost reputation, he rode northwards in 1681, the year following his ignominious defeat at the hands of the Indians. As he moved up the Rio Grande, he found the southern pueblos deserted and, upon arriving at the Isleta Pueblo, he burned part of the village as a punitive measure and took five hundred captives from Isleta and Sandia. Further north, when he encountered a large army of Indians, he prudently decided to beat a hasty retreat to El

Paso. The Isleta prisoners who accompanied him settled in an area east of the town, naming their new pueblo, Isleta del Sur.

Although Otermin's attempt at reconquest proved abortive, the Spanish authorities in Mexico City had no intention of abandoning the province of New Mexico. In the first place, it was repugnant to the Spanish soul to allow thousands of Indian converts to revert to "paganism", since the original missionary motive of the colonization was still operative. But even more important was Spain's fear that France would move into the political vacuum created by an abandoned New Mexico.

Soon after the defeat of Spanish arms, it became clear that Indian unity was largely a myth and had lasted for only a brief period while their common hatred of Spain and her institutions existed. During their temporary solidarity, the Indians missed the opportunity to form a confederacy to consolidate their advantageous position. Instead, the inchoate spirit of unity quickly disintegrated, giving way to the age-old fractiousness and disunity. The various pueblos fell to quarreling among themselves and with the Plains Indians who had briefly been their allies. No policy had been formulated to meet the anticipated Spanish retaliation, and so the ground was laid for the eventual reconquest of New Mexico by Don Diego de Vargas.

In the meantime Indians expressed their hatred in tangible ways by attempting to wipe out all trace of Spain's presence during the past century. Catholic churches were razed, and those couples who had been married by the friars were remarried according to Indian ritual. To erradicate the effects of Catholic baptism, many Indians ritually bathed in the rivers to cleanse themselves of the pollution of the Christian sacrament. Even Spanish technological innovations were scorned; plows and farm implements were smashed to pieces, and the native farmers returned to the use of the traditional dibble stick.

During this period of exile, Governors for the El Paso colony were regularly appointed by the Viceroy. Otermin was succeeded by Domingo Jironaza Petriz de Cruzate, who governed, with one year's interruption, from 1683-1689. He succeeded in reconnoitering the region in 1688 to verify the reports of Indian disunity, but apart from doing battle with the inhabitants of the Zia Pueblo, Cruzate was able to produce few positive results from his venture. The honor of reconquering New Mexico for Spain was bestowed in 1688 on the newly appointed Governor and Captain-General of the colony, Don Diego de Vargas, Zapata, Luxan, Ponce de Leon.

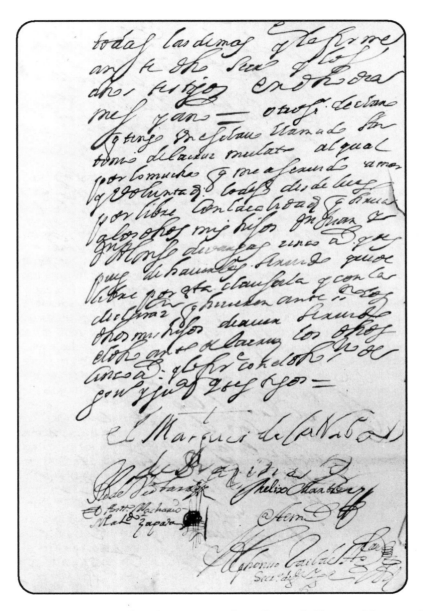

Figure 6: Last Will and testament of Don Diego de Vargas, Marques de la Nava de Brazinas. Spanish Archives of New Mexico 1. No. 1027. New Mexico State Records Center and Archives.

CHAPTER 7

THE RECONQUEST

There exists a myth popular among New Mexicans that the reconquest of the territory by de Vargas was accomplished without bloodshed. Fiesta pageants depict docile Indians falling at the feet of the friars, begging their forgiveness while a magnanimous de Vargas, under the protection of the diminutive statue of 'La Coquistadora,' dispenses largesse and forgiveness to his errant children. The facts prove otherwise.

The new Governor set about the reconquest of New Mexico in two stages. The first "entrada" in August, 1692, was merely a military foray into the north country and no attempt was made to re-settle the colonists. With a small detachment of troops, de Vargas moved up the Rio Grande. Along the way he discovered that the Indians had prior knowledge of his coming and had sought refuge in the mountains which rib the valleys of the Rio Grande. Some deserted pueblos gave mute testimony of the ravages of Apache raids during the absence of Spain's protective military power.

On September 13, 1692, De Vargas rode up to the gates of Santa Fe unopposed. So fragmented were the pueblos at the time that the Tanos, who occupied Santa Fe, had received no forewarning of the arrival of the Spanish. They thought that hostile neighbors were trying to trick them into opening the city gates by posing as Spanish soldiers and they demanded that the troopers fire an harquebus and sound a trumpet to prove that they were indeed the returning Spaniards. The Tanos took heart when they realized how meager was the Spanish force and treated de Vargas with utter disdain. He, in turn, showed the seriousness of his intent by aiming his cannons at the city gate and drawing up his troops in battle array. Only then did the Tanos agree to parley and allow de Vargas to enter the city unarmed in the company of two Franciscan friars. Standing in the central 'plaza,' he fought to control his anger as he beheld the destruction of the capital city. The parish church had been converted into a kiva, its door boarded up and holes bored into the roof to serve as entrances. The Indians had occupied the prosperous houses and buildings surrounding the 'plaza' and whole families had even taken up residence in the Palace of the Governors, symbol of Spain's royal power.

In an eloquent speech, the governor succeeded in convincing the Tanos that they would be treated kindly by their former overlords if they would submit peacefully to his authority. He also claimed jurisdiction from the Spanish King to pardon all past offenses in return for a promise of allegiance to Crown and Church. The Tanos, realizing the futility of continued rebellion, humbly submitted to the Spanish King in the person of his emissary. For the Indians of New Mexico, a golden opportunity for a lasting defiance of Spanish authority had been squandered when they failed to forge strong bonds of unity and singleness of purpose after the successful Pueblo Revolt.

Accompanied by his new allies, the Tanos, de Vargas set about the task of subduing the rest of the pueblos. One group after another was granted amnesty as the Indians once again bowed to Spanish rule. It is calculated that during the first "entrada", de Vargas renewed the allegiance to the Crown of twenty-three pueblos. The clerics who accompanied the expedition claimed to have baptized 2,214 souls, most of them children born since the 1680 insurrection.

A contributing factor to the rapid submission of the Indian pueblos was their disillusionment with their newly acquired freedom. In the first heady weeks of victory, it was easy to slough off the yoke of Spain and to exist happily in a state of euphoria, free from exploitation. But many Indians keenly felt the absence of Spanish agricultural technology, and, as the Plains Indians increased their raids against the pueblos, they sorely missed the protection afforded by Spanish soldiers. Consequently, a large number of Indians supported the return of the colonists as the lesser of two evils.

With his mission in the North accomplished, the Governor returned to El Paso to organize the re-colonization of New Mexico, a process which would turn out to be both lengthy and difficult. The promises which De Vargas had brought with him from the pueblo 'caciques' proved to be ephemeral, as one after the other, realizing the full implications of living under Spain's harsh scepter, withdrew his vows of obedience to de Vargas. Many Pueblo Indians, including the Tanos occupying Santa Fe, decided on armed resistance, and thus, the second "entrada" was destined to be a slow, painstaking and sanguinary process of resettlement which would last till the end of the decade.

But in 1693, the colonists' hopes were high. A news bulletin in the form of a pamphlet entitled "Mercurio Volante", was published by order of the Viceroy to inform the people of New Spain that the reconquest of New Mexico was in progress, "conseguida por Don Diego de Vargas". The writer of the pamphlet was one of the New World's most eminent scholars, Carlos Siguenza y Gongora

The second "entrada" got under way on September 13, 1693. A hardy group of former New Mexican colonists, who had persevered during thirteen years of exile, never giving up hope of one day returning to their homeland, formed the core of families preparing for the march northward. They were accompanied by two young Frenchmen, Jean Archiveque and Jacques Grollet, survivors of La Salle's ill-fated expedition to the Texas coast. In addition, the expedition consisted of one hundred soldiers recruited from New Spain and the Iberian Peninsula. The Church, too, was represented by seventeen Franciscans, eager to rekindle the spark of Faith which their predecessors had ignited in New Mexico.

The returning colonists could boast eighteen wagons, a thousand mules, two thousand horses and nine hundred head of cattle. As they followed the old trail north, they had to contend with the harshness of a bitter winter, and as many as 30 women and children died of exposure 'en route' to Santa Fe. When the caravan finally arrived at the erstwhile capital on December 16, 1693, the colonists found the Tano Indians still in possession of the city. They were forced to make camp outside the city walls, constructing flimsy, makeshift shelters which were hardly adequate to repel the biting cold.

On several occasions the Governor tried to prevail upon the Tanos to return to their pueblo at Galisteo, but they defied his authority, scoffing at him from atop their walled fortress. Meanwhile, the situation in the colonists' shantytown had become desperate as the winter weather held the mountains and valleys in an icy grip. Twenty-two more children had died from exposure; supplies of food and fuel were alarmingly low and disease had begun to ravage the camp.

On December 28, de Vargas ordered a full scale attack on the town. The battle was joined early in the morning and continued for most of the day, but the Spanish were unable to breach Santa Fe's defenses. By mid-afternoon, the governor was forced to suspend his attack on the city and turn his attention to a new threat from the North. Tewa allies appeared on the scene and attacked de Vargas' rear, causing his forces to abandon the assault on the city and to engage the Tewas in fierce fighting. The Governor's ability to deploy his troops effectively in the open soon gave the advantage to the Spanish, who quickly routed the enemy in a series of lightning skirmishes. But the situation in Santa Fe had not changed by nightfall. The Tanos, manning the town walls, repulsed the troopers with rocks, spears and arrows, hurling blasphemies directed at the Virgin Mary and the Saints, a provocation which only served to anger the attackers and strengthen their determination to annihilate the defenders of Santa Fe. Calling on the Blessed Virgin and St. James, the troopers repeatedly stormed the walls, but were constantly repulsed by the defenders. At last, during the night, the attackers succeeded in breeching the defenses and infiltrating the Indian positions. By dawn, their bold move had placed them in control of the town's bastions and their adversaries, realizing all was lost, sued for peace. The governor, however, angry at the insults and blasphemies which the Tanos had hurled at his men, decided to make an effective example of them. Seventy warriors were lined up in the Santa Fe plaza and executed, thereby sending a signal to discourage further rebellion in the pueblos. The remaining Tanos, perhaps as many as 400, were distributed as slaves among the Spanish settlers as spoils of a "just war".

But the bloody reconquest of Santa Fe did not bring peace immediately to troubled New Mexico. In the following year, the Governor was forced to do battle with other recalcitrant pueblos. The Tewas of Santa Clara had sought refuge on top of Black Mesa and managed to hold the Spanish forces at bay for six months until August, 1694. De Vargas also made combat forays against the Cochiti and Jemez Pueblos and against the Utes of the far North who were making hostile inroads into New Mexico.

By the end of the year 1696, the armed resistance of the pueblos had ended and was replaced by a 'modus vivendi' in which the colonists and the native inhabitants lived in comparative harmony, though the two disparate cultures never completely melded and have retained their separate identities to the present day.

The Pueblo Revolt marks one of the grandest gestures of the American Indian to halt the inexorable European encroachment into his lands. Yet inevitably, the attempt failed for lack of follow-through plans to consolidate the advantages of military victories and numerical superiority. And so, by the year 1700, the Kingdom of New Mexico was once again under the control of Spain. As a result of de Vargas' shrewd plans of settlement and consolidation, the resuscitated colony, though never destined to become wealthy, began to prosper.

Now that the threat of rebellion had been laid to rest, the Governor turned his attention to rebuilding the colony's shattered past. A massive building and renovation program was launched; new towns, like Santa Cruz de la Canada, were established, and new colonists from the environs of Mexico City and Zacatecas were given land-grants by the Governor.

In the last decades of the 17th. century, the constant depredations of the Plains' Indians had become a serious problem, which would threaten the fragile peace in New Mexico during the 18th. century. Apaches, Comanches, Navajos and Utes began to escalate their attacks on the scattered pueblos, ranches and townships, running off the livestock, stealing the stores of corn and randomly killing and kidnapping Spaniard and Indian alike. As a result, the Pueblo Indians joined forces with the Spanish militia against their common enemy to become "los indios aliados" (allied Indians), a term used in official documents to distinguish them from the Plains Indians, "los indios barbaros" (barbaric Indians).

Such usage of Indian auxiliaries in the conquest of the New World was by no means a recent innovation. Cortez had conquered the Aztec empire with the help of many tribes discontented with Aztec rule, and later, Tlascalan Indians accompanied Onate's original colonists to New Mexico. Pueblo auxiliaries, loyal to the Crown, had served Spain as interpreters and scouts and were instrumental in helping de Vargas to reconquer the province and to quell the turmoil in northern New Mexico during the reconquest. In the next century, as the attacks of the Plains' Indians reached epidemic proportions, the Pueblo auxiliaries formed a powerful bastion in the defense of New Mexico. The manner in which they served the militia varied. Some were employed as guides to lead the troops on punitive expeditions against hostile Apaches, Comanches and Navajos. As soldiers, they fought alongside the Spanish militia, often accounting for eighty percent of the fighting force.

By mobilizing their Pueblo allies and the local militias, the authorities in Santa Fe devised a method of containing the raids of the Plains Indians within tolerable limits. Generally, news of an attack reached the Governor in Santa Fe through Pueblo scouts located in strategic areas throughout the province. The Governor would immediately call a council of war, "junta de guerra", to decide the best course of action. Taking part in the council were the Pueblo 'caciques' responsible for recruiting the auxiliaries; they were ordered to produce a stipulated number of warriors, arms and materiel. Once the muster had been decided upon, the various groups met at a central mobilization point led by their war captains , "los capitanes majores de la guerra". Under the command of the provincial Governor or one of his representatives, the expedition would set out in pursuit of the marauders. In the early years of these military forays, there was a certain amount of official discrimination against the Indian allies, who were expected to maintain separate camps. But gradually, as mutual confidence and trust grew, both groups integrated and fought side by side in defense of their lands and property. From contemporary accounts of these eighteenth century campaigns, "los indios aliados" acquitted themselves with honor, demonstrating a bravery and military skill which drew praise and admiration from their Spanish mentors. When a campaign was completed, the auxiliaries were demobilized and free to return to their pueblos after sharing the spoils of war, which were divided equally, without discrimination, among the expeditionaries.

Although the over-all success of these eighteenth century sorties against "los indios barbaros" is questionable, they did represent a strategy of containment which would have been impossible to implement without the help of the Pueblo Indians. The "final solution" of the "Indian problem" in the Southwest would have to await the advanced technology of extermination ruthlessly applied by the United States army in the 1870s and 1880's. But more significantly, the common problem faced by New Mexicans during the colonial period forged strong bonds of mutual respect and cooperation among the Indians of the pueblos and the Hispanic population of the region. This new climate of accord originated with de Vargas' reconquest of New Mexico and stands out in sharp contrast to the overt animosity between Spaniard and Pueblo Indian in the 17th, century.

As for the hero of the reconquest, Don Diego de Vargas was not destined during his lifetime to enjoy the encomiums which posterity has showered upon him. Instead, like Onate a hundred years earlier, he suffered from the ingratitude of Spanish officialdom. Shortly after his pacification of the North, his successor, Governor Pedro Rodriguez Cubero, and the "cabildo", the town council of Santa Fe, brought accusations against him. The tenor of these indictments followed the usual pattern: mistreatment of the Indians, mismanagement of the colony and fiscal malfeasance. The ex-Governor was placed under house arrest, deprived of his property and heavily fined. His incarceration lasted three years, during which time much of his work of consolidation and reconstruction came to a halt under the Cubero administration. Both old and new settlers had grown discouraged at the stagnation apparent at all levels throughout the colony.

Eventually, because of the intervention of the Franciscan custodian, Friar Francisco de Vargas, the ex-Governor was finally exonerated. The friar had become disgusted at the manner in which Cubero was mismanaging the colony and had decided to report personally to the Viceroy in Mexico City. In 1700 he made the long and arduous journey to the Capital of New Spain and explained to Viceroy Sarmiento the reasons for the deteriorating affairs in the colony. The result of the friar's efforts on behalf of de Vargas was the latter's immediate reappointment as Governor of New Mexico and the bestowal of the noble title of Marquis.

In 1703, the newly re-instated Governor began his long range programs which would launch New Mexico into the eighteenth century. Far removed from the center of empire, New Mexico would play a role as a buffer against the imperialistic designs of other foreign powers. Spain's policy makers had given up any grandiose designs of an economic bonanza in New Mexico; instead, the province was destined to develop agricultural and pastoral characteristics distinctive to the region. Small subsistence farming and sheep raising provided a hardscrabble livelihood for New Mexicans during these colonial years, creating a socio-economic pattern of rural living which is still characteristic of northern New Mexico today.

The early settlers, whose numbers were gradually augmented by immigration from Mexico, put down deep roots in their adopted lands. Social class distinctions blurred in the frontier environment and a sense of basic equality existed among the pioneers on the Spanish empire's northernmost borders. There was, of course, a considerable number of rich people in the colony, mostly government officials or proprietors of extensive land grants, which supported large-scale farming and ranching. But social distinctions were minimal, and, if indeed there was an aristocracy, it was one of wealth rather than of birth.

Among the Hispanic families of New Mexico, mestization was natural to a people who shared their Spanish forbears indifference to the mingling of ethnic bloodlines. Although Hispanics lived as Europeans and the Pueblo Indians continued to preserve their ancient culture, both groups shared a common frontier experience, wresting the same hard living from the reluctant earth. Thus, after the turmoil of discovery and settlement, the seeds of Hispanic New Mexico's social, cultural and economic characteristics germinated and flowered into a vibrant regional culture that prevails to this day. Although further modifications of New Mexican society would take place later with the arrival of the Anglo-Americans in the nineteenth century, the region still retains its Spanish heritage intact.

Governor de Vargas himself only saw the early stages of the process of consolidation and development of his colony. In March, 1704, while on a raiding expedition against the Apaches, he fell ill and died at Bernalillo.

His remains were brought to Santa Fe, where, in accordance with his request, he was buried under the high altar in the parish church. Masses were said for the repose of his soul, and alms were distributed among the poor on the day of his burial.

With the passing of de Vargas, New Mexico's long period of gestation was over and the history of discovery and conquest finally came to an end. In an age of empire builders, with its super-heroes like Cortez and Pizarro, Vasco da Gama and Magellan, who conquered the seas and scaled the mountains, the feats of Coronado, Onate and de Vargas might pale by comparison. But they were men cast from the same Iberian mold, and only chance, time and place determined their lesser role in history. Yet they, too, were giants astride an exciting age of discovery.

An Early History Of The American Southwest 61

INDEX